ORLEANS INN

A Cape Cod Legend

Front Cover

This original painting by Jack Kitson
Titled: ORLEANS INN est.1875
is of Captain Aaron Snow and his crew arriving on his schooner the Nettie M. Rogers at the wharf of the Orleans Inn.

Credit: Jack Kitson
Kitson Fine Arts
Studio/Gallery
P.O. Box 691
20 Massasoit Road
Eastham, MA 02642

508-255-6426

ORLEANS INN
A Cape Cod Legend

PASSENGERS ON THE MAYFLOWER

"The names of those which came over first, in the year 1620, and were by the blessing of God the first beginners and in a sort the foundation of all the Plantations and Colonies in New England; and their families."

John Carver and Katherine, his wife. Desire Minter and two manservants, *John Howland*, Roger Wilder. William Latham, a boy. A maidservant and a child that was put to John Carver called Jasper More.

William Brewster and **Mary**, his wife; their two sons, **Love** and **Wrestling**. A boy that was put to him called **Richard More**, and his sister, Mary. The rest of the Brewsters' children were left behind but came later.

Edward Winslow and Elizabeth, his wife. Two manservants called ***George Soule*** and Elias Story; also, a little girl was put to him called Ellen, the sister of Richard More.

William Bradford and his wife, Dorothy. The Bradfords had one son who remained behind but came on a later ship.

Isaac Allerton and his wife, Mary, and their three children, **Bartholomew**, **Remember**, and **Mary**. And a servant boy named John Hooke.

Samuel Fuller and a servant called William Button. Samuel Fuller's wife and their child came afterwards.

John Crackstone and his son, **John Crackstone**.

Captain Myles Standish and Rose, his wife.

Christopher Martin, his wife, Marie and two servants, Solomon Prower and John Langmore.

William Mullins, his wife Alice, and their two children, Joseph and **Priscilla**; as well as a servant, Robert Carter.

William White and his wife, **Susanna**, and their son, **Resolved**, and a son born aboard ship, called **Peregrine**. Also, two servants named William Holbeck and Edward Thompson.

Stephen Hopkins and **Elizabeth**, his wife, and their two children, **Damaris** and **Oceanus**; the latter was born at sea. Also, Stephen Hopkins' children from his first marriage, **Giles** and **Constance**. And two servants called ***Edward Doty*** and *Edward Lester*.

Richard Warren. His wife and children were left behind but came later.

John Billington and his wife **Elinor**, and their two sons, **John** and **Francis**.

Edward Tilley and Ann, his wife, and two children that were their cousins **Henry Sampson** and **Humility Cooper**.

Names in *italic* indicate the signers of the Mayflower Compact; names in bold letters indicate those who survived the first year.

John Tilley and his wife, Joan, and **Elizabeth**, their daughter.

Francis Cooke and his son, **John**. Francis Cooke's wife and other children came afterwards.

Thomas Rogers and **Joseph**, his son; his other children came afterwards.

Thomas Tinker, his wife, and a son.

John Rigdale and his wife, Alice.

James Chilton, his wife, and their daughter, **Mary**. Their other daughter, who was married, came later.

Edward Fuller, his wife and **Samuel**, their son.

John Turner and two sons. He had a daughter who came some years later to Salem.

Francis Eaton and Sarah, his wife, and **Samuel**, their son, a young child.

Moses Fletcher. His wife, Sarah, and his children remained in Holland.

Digory Priest. His wife, Sarah, and children stayed behind in Holland. Sarah, with the knowledge of her husband's death, married Godbert Godbertson. The family came to New Plymouth in 1623.

John Goodman.

Thomas Williams, *Edmund Margesson*, ***Peter Browne***, *Richard Britteridge*, *Richard Clarke*, ***Richard Gardiner***, ***Gilbert Winslow***.

John Alden was hired as a cooper at Southampton where the ship was supplied. Left to his own liking to go or stay, he decided to stay and married in New Plymouth.

John Allerton and *Thomas English* were both hired. The latter to master a shallop in the new colony; the other was reputed as one of the company but was to go back (being a seaman) for the help of others behind. However, they both died before the ship returned.

There were also two other seamen hired to stay a year in the colony, **William Trevor** and one Ely, but when their time was out they both returned to England.

ADAPTED FROM:
William Bradford
Of Plymouth Plantation 1620-1647
Samuel Eliot Morison, editor
1970 (Alfred A. Knopf, New York)

Plimoth Plantation
P.O. Box 1620
Plymouth, MA 02362
(508) 746-1622 x 332 (Mail Order)
(800) 262-9356 x 332 (Mail Order)
www.plimoth.org

To the families, friends and guests
of the Orleans Inn

This book is dedicated to the families past and present who have preserved the wonderful structure and kept its legend alive. Our appreciation is extended to those that have supported the Inn in the past and those that will assure its presence in the future.

Your support can best be provided by visiting the Inn and sharing in its history.

Shannon and Javier on their wedding day
June 23,2003
St Joan of Arc Church
Orleans, MA

Parents, Ed and Laurie Maas
Brothers, Shawn, Ryan, Logan
Sisters, Megan, Caitlin, Erin
(not shown Brandon)

PREFACE

This book is intended to give the reader a perspective of a wonderful old Victorian sea Captain mansion and what was involved in salvaging it unlike so many others that have been razed. Some background has been laid to give insight to the thought process and Divine intervention in the perceived impossible task of rescuing the old building.

A spiritual aspect is inevitable as the only thing that kept us going was our Judeo-Christian faith. Although Laurie is a conservative New England Protestant and Ed is a devout Roman Catholic they have raised eight children to respect all religions and faiths.

Father Richard Roy performed a blessing of the Inn for the 125th anniversary on May 15, 2000. He has been an inspiration since the Maas family acquired the Inn and performed the wedding ceremony for their oldest daughter Shannon on June 23rd, 2003.

This book is a compilation of thoughts and occurrences over the course of 130 years the Inn has existed. The Inn enjoyed the Victorian period and suffered during the Great Depression and Prohibition. Please visit the Inn to immerse yourself in its richness.

Captain Aaron Snow
1827-1892
Descendent of Constance Hopkins, teenage passenger on Mayflower. Built Orleans Inn 1875

CHAPTER 1

ORLEANS INN

A Cape Cod Legend

Constance Hopkins was peering over the bow of the Mayflower and caught a glimpse of a speck on the horizon. She cautiously whispered to her father Stephen and brother Giles to focus on the enlarging dot. The thirteen year old precocious child was witnessing the arrival of her fellow pilgrims to a new and strenuous life.

The Nauset Highlands were looming in the distance and the seals and seagulls were frolicking in the surf. They observed the futile attempts of the weary crew attempt the southern route to Jamestown. After nearly grounding on the treacherous Chatham Shoals they reversed directions and rounded the tip of Province Lands. After anchoring in the protected harbor, search parties were dispatched to find a suitable encampment.

After the first encounter with the Nauset Indians the Mayflower headed west to the site of the first New England settlement of Plymouth. Half of the passengers perished the first winter. The remaining 52 settlers were very hardy and established a foothold in the new colony. The Anne arrived three years later and Constance was smitten by a strong young man arriving named Nicholas Snow. They were married and became one of seven families to settle what is now known as Cape Cod.

Nicholas and Constance settled the Nauset area that is now the town of Orleans. Their descendants were integral in the fabric of the community. The heart of the Cape is now the Orleans Rotary. Constance is buried in the Old Cove burying ground. The monument to her heritage remains just the other side of the rotary and is known as the Orleans Inn. A number of Snow generations established a strong and vibrant community. Isaac Snow fought against the British to help establish independence in the newly created United States. He and his fellow soldiers were captured and sent to Portugal on prison ships. They escaped and were given shelter and passage from the French.

The Duke of Orleans had visited the area of the Cape when escaping the French Revolution. Isaac had been influential on his return in naming the newly created town which had been part of Eastham. In an effort to thumb their nose at the British the only town created after the revolution was named after Orleans, France. The French transatlantic cable was brought to the area and the French Cable museum stands a short walk from the Orleans Inn.

The descendant of Isaac Snow born in 1827, Aaron Snow, became a sea captain and acquired the Nettie M. Rogers sailing vessel. He had inherited a large parcel on the protected harbor of town cove. He began building a wharf to handle the increasing amount of goods brought in by ship. He built a warehouse on the site. Aaron then began the most ambitious project of his life which became a testament to his famous family. The six story structure began rising on the shore adjacent to the bustling activity of the shipping wharf. The community watched with wonder at the huge structure which would become the beautiful Victorian mansion completed in 1875 for the Snow family. Captain Snow and his wife Mary and their seven children established a lasting presence.

The main floors of the home were transformed to the store to handle the increasing trade from the wharf. The rail was becoming more utilized in the transport of heavy materials so the store was moved to its current location on Main Street adjacent to the rail depot. The same Snow family own and operate the store which is a testament to the family. Captain Aaron Snow and his wife Mary passed away within weeks of each other in 1892.

The home was vacant for eight years until the Snow family sold it for $1000 at the turn of the century. Two older ladies who were sisters purchased the property and opened it as a guest house and stagecoach stop for weary travelers. A number of families had purchased and sold the property until it was expanded into a luxury hotel in the late 1940's. This was at a time that many returning soldiers from World War II had become involved in the construction and expansion of older properties.

It is ironic that it was a German, Bruno Burkhart, that was responsible for the creation of the modern day hotel and resort. He oversaw the expansion and reformation into a classic hotel. He named the expansive dining room the Brunella room after him and his wife. The deck was extended over the water and hosted many celebrities including movie stars.

The main level was extended to accommodate a large professional kitchen. The aft deck was built to provide a tavern which is popular year round. Fourteen hotel rooms were constructed on the upper level with a beautiful staircase leading to the lodging area.

The hotel was sold to a Greek immigrant Demitri Stamatis. He also acquired the Captain Linnell house and was involved in an auto accident traveling between the two. He sold the Inn to the Martin family and Eddie was a legend in his time. The Martin children decided not to continue with the business and it was sold to the Costa/Servidio family. Off Cape acquisitions by Joe Servidio were draining the Inn of needed resources and it fell into disrepair. The bank took control of the Inn and sold it to the Sutphin family. The property was soon foreclosed and sold at auction. The winning bid was $410,000 and the bidder could not come up with the money within the required 30 days. The bank kept the $10,000 deposit and listed the property with American Heritage Realty. The town had conducted studies on the property and most had recommended raising the structure. It almost became a parking lot connecting town landing and the historic windmill park.

The building was abandoned when Ed first walked through Memorial Day weekend. The ceiling collapsed as Ed was being told it could reopen for the season. Ed swore he would never own a restaurant.

Ed signed the offer and gave a deposit that day. He could not sleep and went to Nauset Beach to watch the sunrise at 3AM. There was one lone person huddled in the lifeguard stand. He shared his secret with Wilson Farrar.

The building was purchased with a contract finalized in the summer of 1996 by Ed Maas.

Fred and Kay Maas
Married in 1948

CHAPTER 2

THE MAAS FAMILY

In 1926 Fred Maas was born in Chicago. He was one of 9 children, two of which died in infancy. Fred was not a well child and his parents allowed him to pursue his love of birds, converting their garage into a pigeon coop. He acquired a partnership in Larry&Lou's tavern on the South Side when his older brother Larry went to serve the Army in WWII. He moved his family to FL and became involved in agricultural research for the University of Florida in the Redlands. He is known today as an expert on tropical trees.

Kathleen O'Hagan was born in County Down Ireland and moved to Chicago as an infant. She met and married Fred Maas 57 years ago. She was employed by the New York Times, Chicago office and worked for the Sandoz Company in Homestead, FL.

Ed was the third of seven children and was the first to be born in FL. His older sister Carol assisted with the purchase of the Inn and is a teacher in FL. His older brother Fred is a police Chief with Sunny Isles Beach, FL. Ed was chairman of the South Florida Hospital Association.

Ed began his health care career at the hospital where he was born. James Archer Smith now known as Homestead Hospital is in the process of being replaced with a modern facility. At the age of 16 Ed left the fields of the Redlands in South Florida doing manual labor for 50 cents an hour and worked in the hospital kitchen making $1.25 an hour mopping floors in the kitchen. He worked every day after high school and the next year began working in Central Supply and then Respiratory Therapy. When Ed left for college he was asked to find a replacement and saw the perfect candidate in his sister Kathy. When Kathy went to college she recommended her sister Martha who today runs the Cardiac Stress lab at Homestead Hospital. Rose also became a nurse and now manages a surgery center. John became the most prominent attorney in Homestead.

I tried to visit my family in Homestead whenever I could. They thought I was crazy for the impulsive decision to buy the Inn. I tried to allay their concerns by saying that if the Inn was knocked down as recommended the land was worth more without the building.

I then tried to find some possible healthcare use for the building such as an ACLF. Now these possibilities were not practical but there was no way that I would ever admit to planning to run it as a restaurant. The old adage of "how do you turn a lot of money into little money" still rang true. "Just buy a restaurant".

I was in the family living room with my parents talking about the purchase and sales agreement. My Dad thought I was nuts as he owned a Tavern in Chicago. He went over all the problems with shakedowns from officials to theft from trusted employees. I thought these problems were in the past. I had only put up the $5,000 deposit but was seriously considering moving ahead. The week later I had to put up another $35,000 when the offer was accepted. I called my brother John and asked for his advice. His legal advice was that I had to make my own decision. He stated that if I did not consummate the deal I would lose the $40,000 deposit. I went to the bank and set up a line of credit for the Maas Group and sent the check. I was now under the gun to come up with $365,000 in just 2 weeks. I called my investment broker and asked about cashing in my retirement 401k accounts. Dan Kucera told me to keep the accounts in place and he would draw a percentage loan against them and wire the funds to the bank. We were still about $200,000 short and the deal was going to fall through. I flew up to the closing and told the Realtor I needed more time. Tom Cronin drove me to the Barnstable Courthouse where we found our attorney Herb Roberts. He joked with us as we nervously enter the foyer. I asked him what happened. He said I had another month to come up with the money. He had arrived early and met with the bank that was selling the Inn. I asked him how he was able to get the extension and he said they were not too happy. They could have easily kept the $40,000 deposit as they had with the failed auction deposit. I asked what reason he gave them for the delay and he said I just told them "shit happens". I was so relieved I grabbed his hand and thanked him.

Again back in FL, I sought refuge in my parent's living room. I was talking to my Dad who had his money tied up in bonds and could not help. I had asked CCB&T for a line of credit as they were handling the wire transfers. Since I had no relationship with them that was not going to happen. My Dad still thought I was crazy. He kept reminding me. He said that my sister Carol had savings bonds that he thought she should invest. I got up and called her to tell her of my hairbrained idea. She is very trusting and I asked her to talk to her husband Nelson prior to answering. She called back and said I could use them to close the deal. What a burden was lifted off my shoulders. I met Carol and her daughter Kathleen at a bank in Fl and we wired the funds to CCB&T. The lawyers were to handle everything from that point. It was now July 1996 and the children were at our summer home in East Orleans. They taught swimming for the Town of Orleans and were told not to say a word about the purchase. Rumors were swirling around town that the Inn was being sold to Chili's. I called the realtor and asked where that was coming from and he just said it was a small town. Laurie and I were driving up from FL and did not know whether the Inn was ours or not. We arrived late on a Thursday night and called Tom the first thing in the morning.

He congratulated us as the new owners of the Orleans Inn and said he would meet us at the Inn at noon with the keys. It was the first time Laurie had seen the Inn. The expression on her face was, "What in the world did he do this time?" She was not impressed and certainly not amused. "So what are you going to do with it?" She asked.

"I don't know" Ed answered which was not very reassuring.

The children were finally able to disclose that our family had bought the Inn to cries of "Are you crazy? The place is haunted". The matter had somehow not been mentioned in the process. I called Tom and he said he had heard some rumors. "Rumors?" There were newspaper articles written about the ghosts of the Orleans Inn. We decided to return at night with the kids and gave them flashlights as there was no power nor water. Their courage started to fade with the batteries and dwindling light. They did make it to the Cupola and thought is was kind of neat. No ghost sightings this time, however.

Some weeks later Laurie was showing our neighbor, Natalie around the boarded up Inn. In the hallway on the lodging level both froze in their tracks. They had felt a cold blast of air from nowhere and thought it must be the ghost seeking their warmth. Laurie decided at that instant to save the Inn for the ghost. When she told me I thought the bank is going to love that justification for requesting a loan. She actually had a plan.

While driving back with the children to FL, Ryan asked Laurie if he could take the Inn on as a project. He had just graduated from high school and was working at a Maroone Auto dealership. Mom said that if he promised to go to Cape Cod Community College she would talk to Dad. Ed agreed to set up a line of credit at the bank for renovations and Ryan moved into the summer home. The agreement was that the entire project would come in at $200,000 including start up costs. Looking back this was unrealistic.

Ryan moved to the Cape on his own and registered at the college. Ed brought up the 94 Chevy Impala Super Sport for him to drive. Ryan's first class at the community college was with the Dean of the Program. He asked what the students background in hospitality was and Ryan said his family just bought the Orleans Inn. In front of class the professor told him "It would be a miracle to do anything with the Orleans Inn". Instead of breaking his spirit that comment drove Ryan to prove him wrong. Ryan worked tirelessly to complete his class work and renovate the Inn.

Ed visited in September and was pulling weeds in front of the building. He was approached by a young man who said he was a chef. He said his wife was an innkeeper and they had a baby. He asked if he could take over management of the Inn when it opened and his wife would run the Inn and he would be the chef. They needed housing so they would move into the upstairs family apartment. Ed bought the story hook, line and sinker. After finding out the truth and background Ryan called Ed in FL and said there were major problems. Ryan was told to deal with it and the first major mistake was corrected. This was our first taste of the other side of the Cape visitors do not see.

Ed looked in the phone book and found what he thought was a reputable name for a contractor to fix the leaking roof. Ed was told by the contractor that the roof had to be replaced but it could not be done without replacing the siding. Ed asked for a bid with both options. The following day the contractor returned with a bid for $50,000 not breaking it down nor giving the option requested. Ed asked when payment was required. The contractor said when the job is done. Ed asked what happened if the job was not done correctly. The contractor said he would not get paid. Ed shook his hand and left for FL. This was a major mistake and the second critical error made by Ed that month.

Ed had received recommendations for a restaurant equipment supplier and an electrician from a friend in the business whom had just completed renovations. Ed hired both resulting in the third and fourth major mistakes in the process. So far he was batting zero.

The building inspector called Ed to tell him the contractor was unlicensed and uninsured. Ed was mortified and asked the contractor who denied the claims. Ed believed him and lived to regret it. The Inn was red tagged several times requiring the engagement of Architect Design to oversee the project. They were a Godsend. By the time Ed found out about the contractor flaws he was in deep trouble. The contractor was paid $20,000 more than the contract and demanded to proceed with the interior. When Ed told him he would not get that contract he tried to stop the project. He took all the windows out and kicked the doors open and said "Let the place freeze". Two workers quit on the spot and returned to replace the windows to protect the Inn from the winter weather. Ryan returned from school and found out what had happened. They told Ryan they would finish the job for materials and labor.

The contractor saw them fixing the damage and called Ed to demand $20,000 and he would "go away." Ed refused to give in to the extortion attempts. The contractor brought the building inspector to the Inn and showed him structural changes he had made and covered up. The building was red tagged again. The contractor called Ed on his anniversary December 16, 1996 and told him the Inn would never reopen and he hoped it was worth $20,000. Resulting litigation was ruled in Ed's favor but it almost ruined him.

The electrical contractor demanded huge amounts of money or the project would be shut down. Ed reminded him the cost was already four times the estimate but that did not seem to matter. Ed left and called his father for the first time in his life asking for money. Ed was crying as his dad told him he thought he had bit off more than he could chew. Ed agreed and was amazed when his Dad came up with the $35,000 to get things moving.

Ryan and Shannon Maas
Opening of the Orleans Inn, May 15, 1997

CHAPTER 3

OPENING DAY

"Dad, bring a cash drawer when you come up", Ryan said to Ed on his cell phone as Ed was driving to the airport. "Ryan, what is a cash drawer?' asked Ed. "Just bring a lot of small bills to make change, I think we are opening this afternoon!" as Ryan hung up.

Ed was late as it was and diverted to the bank which was closest to the airport. He had one last retirement account which was intact and had no option but to cash it in. He found a sympathetic manager and she quickly converted the last of his 401k to small bills. Ed expressed his appreciation as he stuffed the bills into his canvas bag feeling this must be what a drug dealer does and felt very uncomfortable. He was very self conscious boarding the plane with $3,000 in small bills. His mind kept racing ahead in anticipation of the much awaited opening of the Orleans Inn. He was worried for Ryan and felt it was unfair such a young person had to deal with such a huge responsibility.

Trying to hurry for the flight, Ed's cell phone kept ringing with questions from clients. He tried to manage his healthcare consulting business while assisting Ryan with the Inn. He just made the Delta Flight and was happy he was on the right flight. Twice in the past he was in a hurry and boarded the wrong flights only to learn after takeoff. He also missed several flights due to his hectic schedule. Upon landing in Logan he rushed to the Plymouth & Brockton Bus pickup for the trip to Cape Cod. Ed had left his 66 Mustang convertible at the Park&Ride in Barnstable. He was happy that it started as it always had for the ten years he owned it and was on his way. Pushing the speed limit his cell phone went off and it was Ryan.

"Dad, hurry up! I got a temporary partial certificate of occupancy and we have our first customer and I can't make change." "Ryan, just tell them it is on the house and I will be there as soon as I can. I'm driving as fast as I can and will be there soon." Pulling off the Route 6 Rotary a panic set over Ed as he saw cars in the parking lot. A mix of emotions ran over him as he ran into the back door giving Ryan the bag of cash.

Ryan handed me the $5 bill that he received from our first customer. Dad, the customer was Herb Harrison from the fish market and when I told him it was on the house he signed the bill and gave it back to me. I didn't tell him we could not make change. I used my last change for phone calls from the college to the town hall. I told him we would frame the bill and never forget how close we were to not making it.

Ed had told Ryan to put up open signs if he were able to secure a permit. Ryan had taped up a small open sign he had bought at the hardware store. It was a simple paper sign that you could not see from any distance. It was enough to signal the rebirth of the Inn and word was soon out that the Orleans Inn was back in business. Word spread fast and the pub and dining room soon filled up. The computers were still being programmed when the customers started to arrive. The technician became nervous and dumped the whole system. He had to start reprogramming and the staff went to the archaic paper system. The customers never noticed but confusion reigned in the kitchen. The system was brought up again but was sending food orders to the bar instead of the kitchen. The bartender was just throwing the orders in the trash as they were not drink orders. Ryan went to find out what was happening to the orders and pulled a stream of paper from the trash in the bar. He ran to the kitchen and started barking orders to make up for lost time.

The kitchen was in a state of chaos as the chef had never managed a team before. Ryan began orchestrating things as there was a void of leadership. Ed was concerned the chef would walk out and told Ryan to concentrate on the front of the house. This was fatal error as it undermined Ryan's authority and treated him as a son and not a manager. This was the first of a chain of actions which ultimately led Ryan to leave and establish his reputation with several outstanding Boston based restaurant management groups.

The irony was that Ed protected the chef in spite of the failures and lack of responsibility. The chef was carried at a significant salary only to show up occasionally and infrequently. He did little the first winter and the Inn suffered staggering losses. As soon as the spring approached he demanded a huge increase in salary or he would leave. Ryan accepted his resignation and took over the operations. He hired a cook who had some serious psychiatric issues and walked off the job. For several years we were subjected to harassing and threatening phone calls. We then had a cook who showed up drunk and also demanded outrageous increases in salary. We hired a sous chef as an executive chef who almost put us out of business. It was the most miserable two years of business losses.

Ed filled in until the twins could finish their Master's Degree and Josh could return from Florida. There were days that Ed was the bartender, cook and server. That was a long cold winter and thankfully just manageable until relief arrived each weekend. Erin and Megan traveled from Graduate school in Providence and took over for Dad.

Today the Inn is one of the most successful on the Cape. Erin, Megan and Josh serve up to 1,000 guests a day and never have a complaint. It is so gratifying to see them manage so well as they truly worked their way through every position at the Inn.

That first day of opening was so intimidating to Ed that he stayed in the kitchen scraping dishes preparing them for the dishwasher. This position kept him busy and away from anyone finding out that he had no idea what was going on out front. Ryan made a confident presence with the guests and was very personable. Ed did venture out to the dining room and happened to see the reporter that had covered the purchase having dinner. He went over to say hello and she asked if she could put a small announcement in the Cape Cod Times. That little blurb by Susan Milton filled the restaurant for the weeks to come. She has remained a respected friend and is an outstanding reporter.

At the end of the night everyone was exhausted and Ryan said "Dad I don't think we should open for lunch tomorrow. Ed went ballistic as he was pushing for breakfast, lunch and dinner a feat that he now admits was unreasonable. Ryan relented and we opened at 11AM the next day. The view of the water is spectacular and the window tables are very popular. Ed spent most of his time talking with the customers and time after time they said they were "drawn to the building". There is something about the Inn that is magical and mystical. That Friday night a prominent attorney sought me out to tell me that everybody in town that was anyone was at the bar. The bar was 3 to 4 deep packed and it was wild.

That weekend was an incredible adrenaline high and is remembered fondly. Ed was warned by the police that the tone would be set the first week. Ed stood watch at the front door and made sure that if anyone had been drinking elsewhere all day they were not welcome at the Inn. It was amazing how soon the word got out that it was not the sleazy operation that had plagued the final days of previous failures. The clientele today is wonderful and is more like family than guests. They make it all worthwhile.

The Inn was featured in the corporate annual report for the Royal Bank of Scotland. They are the third largest bank in the world and the report was distributed worldwide. Photographers and graphic designers were sent from Scotland to capture the essence of the Inn for the report. Ed and Megan were invited to tour the home bank in Edinborough.

William Dowd of the Albany Times Union writes about the Inn and we greet many visitors from the tri city area. It is always good to see Bill and his family. The Inn has been featured in USA Today and Frommers as well as many nationally distributed books.

CHAPTER 4

CAPE COD

Thoreau visited and wrote about this part of the Cape. Beston wrote the Outermost House and actually stayed at the Inn when his wife came to visit. It is thought that many famous writers, actors, musicians and politicians frequented the Inn. I was told recently that Frank Sinatra's parents frequented the Inn and that Elizabeth Taylor and Montgomery Cliff had been spotted in the 50's. More recently a call from People magazine reporter asked to confirm a rumor that Jennifer Anniston and Brad Pitt were dining at the Inn. Honestly I am so oblivious that the president could be here and I would not know. The kids called a few years back that a reservation was made for the Governor on Mothers Day. They thought it was a prank but I told them it most likely was true and to treat him the same as any other guest. They did and he appreciated the anonymity.

The Cape is a special place not like anywhere else. My own special retreat is Fort Hill Area, the beginning of the National Seashore. It is five minutes from the Inn and is a magnificent place. Drive up to the top of the hill where you will see a panoramic expanse of the town cove, Nauset Inlet and the Atlantic beyond. There are hiking trails that stretch for miles. At the bottom of the hill there are parking areas that lead into the White Cedar Swamp. The boardwalk winds through an area that you would think was the Everglades. There is a microcosm of life that is absolutely amazing. There is a gazebo that is wonderful to stop and relax and read or rest. Continuing on will bring you to the old Indian Sharpening stone. There is also a map and a marker commemorating Champlain's exploration of the area. It is amazing to relive history learned in school as a child.

A guest had stayed in the Inn and told me she was a direct descendant of Constance Hopkins. She was a member of the Snow family and came to visit the Old Cove burying ground. I had driven past the site and only noticed there was a historical marker. After hearing that it was the grave site of Constance I went and discovered a very peaceful and historically significant site. I felt close to Constance and the other Pilgrims buried there.

I was excited to look over one day and notice Gavin McCleod dining in the pub. I always enjoyed the Captain Stubing character on the Love Boat and was amazed he was in our Pub. He actually has a significant presence on the Cape and is a wonderful guy.

One day our daughter Shannon came over and said she thought Maya Angelou was dining in the formal dining room. Sure enough the reservation was made under a different name and then changed to Angelou just before arrival. Her sing song voice was very distinctive and we were so honored to meet her. Everyone was mesmerized by her stories.

Ed had grown up near Key Largo in Homestead Florida. He invited Laurie to go to Rock Harbor, a favorite fishing spot his Dad brought the children to on weekends. Laurie looked at him and said "I grew up spending summers in Rock Harbor". But it was the Cape Cod Rock Harbor an area Ed was not familiar with in the least. Ed brought Laurie to the Everglades for frog legs and she brought him to the Cape for clams. They still have fond memories of their own Rock Harbor but both feel closer to the Cape today than anywhere. Sunsets at Rock Harbor are a favorite of the guests at the Orleans Inn.

Ed met Laurie early in 1972, they began dating in May and were married in December. Ed had to get his parents permission as he was only 19 then turning 20 in September. He had never seen snow and enjoyed his first trip to Cape Cod in October. He was taught by Laurie how to dig for clams and enjoy strolls on the beach. After their Honeymoon they visited Laurie's parents in Braintree and Ed saw his first snowfall. Laurie's cousin brought them to Maine for snowmobiling and Ed thought he was going to die from cold.

Laurie and her parents and sister boarding a boat at Goose Hummock with Orleans Inn in background, 1955.

They always visited the Cape for a few days in summer as Ed was teaching College. The children loved Nauset Beach as well as Skaket. After the twins were born they bought a camper and spent a week and then up to two weeks camping on the Cape. The entire year was anchored by the vacation to the Cape. In 1985 they bought a home in East Orleans. Ed started a summer off program for nurses at the hospital and Laurie was able to spend time at the Cape with the children. Ed visited when he could.

They happened to find the Chatham Band concert on a Friday evening and have enjoyed them for over 20 years. You know everything is right when it is Band Time in Chatham.

Ed was told by a guest of the beauty of Fort Hill Area. He remembers driving past the sign near the Inn but had never taken the time to visit. It is now his favorite escape on the Cape. The boardwalk through the swamp is amazing.

Sunsets in Rock Harbor are like no others. Watch the fishing fleet come in with their daily catch with the setting sun over the horizon. The only other place that comes close is Mallory Square in Key West. There are similarities between the Keys and the Cape.

Nauset Beach is one of the most beautiful beaches in the world. The waves are great for body surfing and the sand is perfect. Orleans manages this part of the National

Seashore. Chatham and Orleans jointly manage the South beach stretching for miles. There are some dune shacks which have been in the same family for generations. Permits are available to drive four wheel vehicles and are very popular in reaching remote areas.

The bike trail on the Cape follows the Old Colony rail beds. When the railroad stopped operating it was decided to pave them over with an extensive bike path. It is very popular for hiking and bicycling through undisturbed areas. The trail is accessible from Canal road across the street from the Inn. The new bridge spans route 6 to make crossing safe. The trail winds through the marsh to the Seashore and is magnificent. The trail in the opposite direction takes you through the Nickerson State Park and beautiful forests. There are bike rental facilities along the way that also do repairs if needed.

Nauset Middle School is within walking distance and just beyond Main Street on Rt. 28. The grounds are the site of the famous Orleans Cardinals Baseball Field and great summer entertainment by the Cape Cod League. Enjoy watching the boys of summer slug it out at the beautiful Eldredge Field. The games are free and offer a great view of the field. There are many Art, Craft and Antique shows at the Middle school as well as concerts and Marine Corps Band presentations. Pops in the Park is one of the best on the Cape. The Spirit of America Marching Band and Gloria de Artes is world renowned and as part of the Community of Jesus in Rock Harbor put on incredible performances at the park. The music and plays presented at the Community are nationally acclaimed.

Stop by one of the historic cemeteries to get a feel of what it must have been like to be an early settler to the Cape. The headstones tell many stories. The ages indicate the very difficult life and treacherous vocations of the sea. Study the names and track them back to the early Mayflower Pilgrims. It is amazing to see such concrete illustration of history.

The Fourth of July is special in Orleans. The Community is a big part of the celebration and the rich history is evident. The entire town turns out for the parade which stretches for miles. The fireworks are some of the best on the Cape and can be viewed from the porch of the Inn. A better vantage point is the Cupola being the tallest structure in town.

Fall for Orleans is a great celebration. There is a great pet parade and the chamber always does something special to celebrate the season. Christmas in Orleans is a wonderful celebration. It falls just after Thanksgiving Day with a special arrival of Santa by boat on the Town Cove. Celebrations include a candlelight caroling stroll and pictures with Mrs. Claus. The town children turn out in droves and it is the best time of year. Megan volunteers her time with this festive event.

Southward Inn

CHAPTER 5

SEA CAPTAINS

Sea Captains of Cape Cod were the wealthy upper class in the Victorian period. The massive mansions were constructed from the wealth of their bounty. Captain Aaron Snow owned the land around the Cove and began building the most historically significant structure in the area. As the structure took shape and rose six stories to remain today the tallest building in the area it was dubbed Aaron's Folly. Captain Snow resided in the home with his wife Mary and their seven children. The main floor of the Inn became the general store for the town. The Inn became the center of commerce for the entire area.

Captain Snow made many trips to Boston on his schooner the Nettie M. Rogers. It took as long to enter the inlet and Cove as it took to make the trip to Boston. The tides hampered the easy navigation in the ever changing channel. Many sailors were needed to guide and nudge the ship into the inlet.

Captain Snow built a wharf behind the Inn to facilitate the unloading of cargo. The timber used to construct the wharf was salvaged from shipwrecks off the treacherous Nauset shoals. Aaron then built storage buildings adjacent to the Inn.

The Inn was built so high in order to give the family a vantage point to view the ship coming in from the ocean. The family in turn placed a tree in the cupola to signal a welcome to the captain and his crew. This tradition continues today at the Orleans Inn.

Ed visits the grave of the Snow family and tells Captain Snow that he is taking care of the wonderful structure he built in 1875. He marvels at what it must have been like for Mary to mother seven children in such a difficult time. The children and their ages make Ed think of the similarities with his family. He was about the same age when he bought the Inn as Captain Snow was when he built the Inn. His oldest son was the same age as Ryan when he oversaw the renovations. He wonders if they had the same experiences and challenges. The obelisk marking the graves is a fitting tribute to the seagoing entrepreneur. He must have been a prominent figure in the community.

Many of these wonderful old sea captain mansions were razed in the interest of expediency. The history can never be replaced. The old Southward Inn was demolished in the 1970's and it can never be replaced. It was a magnificent place and the only remnants left are pictures of the beautiful structure.

Laurie remembers having dinner there as a child with her family after her grandfather's funeral. It is amazing how certain situations like this stay with you a lifetime. She is sad to see the site of the old structure with a modern bank building as the land was worth more without the historic structure. We have postcards of the Southward at the Inn.

Orleans Inn, circa 1900
Home of Sea Captain Aaron Snow
Abandoned in 1892 until it was sold for $1000.00 in 1900.
Orleans Historical Society

CHAPTER 6

THE ABANDONED SNOW HOME

1892 was a year of sadness for the Snow family. Aaron and Mary passed away within weeks of each other. Ed realized this when he visited the cemetery in East Orleans. He heard from a guest that Constance Hopkins was buried in the Old Cove Burying Ground five minutes from the Inn just the other side of the Rotary. After visiting and realizing that Constance and her brother Giles lived to a ripe old age he decided to look for Aaron Snow. He found the family site at the East Orleans cemetery and spent time thinking about how life was back then. He then placed his hand on the obelisk and talked to Aaron. Looking at the dates of birth and death he tried to fit the pieces together.

One baby named after Aaron died at just a few weeks of age. How devastating that must have been. Back then I am sure it was not uncommon but none the less sorrowful. Aaron and Mary died within weeks of each other in spite of a decade difference in age. They must have been so close in life they could not survive without each other.

For eight years the Inn was abandoned. None of the children lived in the Inn after the death of their parents. No commercial shipping activity took place as it was replaced by the railroad. The building sat vacant and boarded up until 1892 when the Snow family sold it for $1000. Although a handsome sum then it is a fraction of the value today.

The two old ladies that bought the home were sisters. They lived there and ran the home as a boarding house. Imagine what it was like in 1900 when the stage coach brought travelers to the Victorian mansion. The two sisters must have decorated the Inn with lace and comfortable furniture. We have tried to restore the Inn to that period. There were no locks on the doors and the goings on in the roaring 20's must have been very interesting.

Various families owned the Inn in the pursuing years. One family sent us old photographs and ironically their name was Bates. The Ellis family owned the Inn at one time. During Prohibition the Inn was the place where you could obtain bootleg whiskey. The hidden doors built into the walls still exist and they concealed the storage for the contraband.

Kathryn Kleekamp created a beautiful oil painting of the Inn in the Victorian period. It is on display in the main lobby of the Inn. It brings you back in time to that wonderful period where the elegantly dressed ladies and gentleman visited the Inn. The stagecoach is bringing guests to the Inn and the vendors are delivering goods to the kitchen. Picnics are taking place on the grounds. It inspired us to hold a Victorian picnic at the Inn in celebration of the 130th anniversary in May 2005.

The German, Bruno Burkhart and his wife are responsible for the major transformation of the Inn in the late 1940's. Many of the old inns were commandeered as hospitals for the serviceman injured in World War II. They were then renovated after the war with the abundance of labor available with the returning serviceman. It is amazing that the center of the Inn remained intact during the massive expansion. The ending result was 22,000 square feet of luxurious hotel and restaurant accommodations. We were given some tariff rates from that period which was $2 per day. The old hotels at that time were American plan and included meals. The staff was fed at specific times before the guests with whatever was available. If they missed that meal they did not eat. The guests had selections from the menu and elegant service. Fresh local seafood and produce was the order of the day. Across the Old County Road was the massive cranberry bog. It has since been developed but many agree should have been maintained as farming related.

Many staff members were immigrants from Germany and were old world trained in customer service.

The transition to college students occurred over time and they were recruited mainly from the Midwest. We have guests that brought their original letters of employment and tales of traveling across the country by bus. They were given room and board as well as a $15 a week salary for seven days work for all waking hours.

Many romances began at the Inn among the guests as well as the employees. I met a couple who met and married while working at the Inn. They have a successful pediatric practice on the South Shore. He became a pediatrician and she became a nurse.

The Martin family bought the Inn in the 1960's and Ed Martin had quite the reputation as a taskmaster. Most have no idea what it takes to run such an operation, but by all accounts he was a pro. His daughter Robin LeFleur was in the seventh grade when the family bought the Inn and resented moving to a new area from the city. She became a respected teacher at the Nauset Middle School. She was instrumental in recognizing and assisting firefighters families after the 9/11 tragedy. Ironically Robin had Caitlin as a student in the seventh grade when our family bought the Inn. Caitlin had the same issues of relocating and leaving friends. What a Godsend to have Robin as a teacher who understood. Caitlin developed a great respect and affinity for Mrs. LeFleur.

CHAPTER 7

THE OLD MAIDS

"Do you really think this is how Papa would have wanted us to spend his inheritance?" Clara asked her older sister Emma? They had taken the $1000 and purchased the abandoned building from the Snow family. They spent the next few months cleaning and preparing the Inn for accepting weary guests on the stage coach stop.

The new century had dawned and the two sisters were filled with excitement and exhaustion. The Inn was six stories and they concentrated on the guest level on the third floor. The mansard roof level was their quarters and their home so to speak. They had a love for cats and the cats had free roam of the Inn. The calico cat was their favorite and played tricks on the guests. There was no problem with mice or rats even though the building had been abandoned for eight years. So many of the old buildings at that time had been infested with vermin and those close to the water were especially prone.

The main floor of the inn became a congregating spot for the entire area. Hunters brought in their shotguns and collapsed on the easy chairs in front of the roaring fireplace. They usually relaxed with a bottle of whiskey provided by the sisters along with a steaming crock of hot corn chowder and hearth baked bread.

Elegant teas took place for the ladies and became the social activity for the time. The sisters enjoyed these the most and were in awe at how popular their Inn had become. Some boarders became residents of the Inn staying months or even years. The money received went directly to the improvements at the Inn and caring for the cats. The sisters were old maids and had no heirs. The Inn became the most elegant in the area.

Henry Beston was a known author at the time and chose the Inn as the meeting place for his wife during her visit to the area. The dedication of the National Seashore brought out the little known fact that breaks from the Outermost House were spent at the Orleans Inn.

Governor Sargent owned the Goose Hummock Shop next to the Inn and spent many an afternoon thawing by the fire after a day of duck hunting on the Nauset Marsh. To this day hunters and fisherman are occasionally guests of the Inn including the former editor of the Boston Sunday Globe magazine. Nick King enjoyed a waterfront room and many blankets upon his return from his duck hunting expeditions.

More visitors are enjoying kayacking and hiking as well as sailing and biking. Bird watchers enjoy visiting

The Birdwatchers General Store across from the Inn. The birding on the Cape is amazing. The Wellfleet Bay Wildlife sanctuary is a jewel of the Mass Audobon Society. It is just past the last Drive In theater on the Cape in Wellfleet. The Theater serves as an enormous flea market during the days and has many treasures.

Candle pin bowling is still popular with a facility in town next to the Coin Laundry. Some of these are throwbacks to the 50's and it seems like time stopped here on the Cape. Some modern changes have occurred including the intrusion of chain stores.

Most town and county zoning has been restricted to limit development and it has helped. The Cape Cod Commission was established to review large developments in cooperation with local authority. The establishment of the Cape Cod National Seashore by President John F. Kennedy was the single most important factor in preserving the natural beauty of the Cape. It is said that the Kennedy family had receptions at the Inn in the past.

One elderly gentleman stopped in to say he had drinks with Captain Jack at the Pub. I looked inquisitively and he said John Kennedy. He said they had done some PT boat training in Cape Cod Bay. I knew of the Target Ship and maneuvers did take place offshore from Otis Air Force Base. He signed our guest book with reference to JFK.

Some of our favorite guests come to mind and two in particular are Michele and Max who come by limo from

Cambridge. They are some of the most fascinating and knowledgeable people I have ever met. Max knew John Steinbeck personally in California and has intrigued me as he has been my favorite author since I read the Grapes of Wrath in ninth grade. Their dog Fooshie is a very popular guest as well. I brought them to Provincetown and Fort Hill. The stories Max told of his visits over 50 years ago were intriguing. They sent me the entire works of Steinbeck as a gift and they are on display in the lobby as one of my personal treasures. They also gave us the most beautiful star lilies.

The Inn is a gem for attracting the most wonderful guests in the world. The Inn used to be like a United Nations in the morning breakfast in the dining room. Things did change somewhat after 9/11. We had every room cancel as guests could not travel. Our policy has always been no cancellation penalty as things do come up. Well, things were pretty scary but we survived. The Inn actually recovered and we had the best fall ever as people drove to the Inn from all over New England. The Cape is the number one destination for all of New England in the summer but spring and fall are beautiful as well.

When the Inn opened we had no hard and fast rules and that continues today. We had not been in the hospitality business and decide to treat everyone as they were guests in our home. It has proven successful and guests return several times each year. We have no minimum stay and no cancellation penalty. It is the only lodging facility on the Cape that we know of that has this policy. Another perk is that we have never charged for a phone call. Local and long distance are provided complimentary for guests or visitors just stopping in to use the phone. It is gratifying to see the expression of guests when told of this free service. It was actually something that we never got around to doing in spite of the fact we were sold a computer to bill guests for phone charges. We just never used it.

Clifford Gustafson
teaching art to students at Dedham High School

CHAPTER 8

GREAT GATSBY AND THE ROARING 20'S

Don't you dare visit that house of ill repute across the cove! Many men were admonished to stay away from the now infamous place of sin and sex. The Inn had a reputation throughout New England for its rowdy parties and lax atmosphere.

The roaring 20's signaled a bustling economy and no one had any idea the bubble would burst during the great depression. The carefree party like atmosphere bolstered the finances of the Inn and added to its reputation. Many a gentleman conducted his business at the Inn and the families were not allowed. Even to this day stories are told of the raucus activities during the period. Wives were always on the watch for a wandering husband near the Orleans Inn. There were reports of the Irish mob taking over the Inn for periods of time with gambling and other activities. The police seemed to look the other way. Government officials were certainly aware of the activities but did not interfere.

We found a Roaring twenties lamp with a flapper which is in the lobby as a testament to the era. We are sure there must have been some offloading onto the dock of the rumrunners cargo. The revenuers from the government seemed to disappear when a delivery was being made. In order to avoid arrest some cargo was dumped in the Bay for pickup later. We still expect to find some of the "boxfish" at the bottom of the Cove.

Imagine the colorful period of the Inn's history and it is like you are stepping back in time. You can almost hear the laughter and music if you listen closely. The cigar smoke was probably thick and the lighting dim. Today the entire Inn is smoke free.

There was a murder of one of the ladies of the house. We named her Hannah just because we came across that name in the archives in the historical section of the Snow Library. You can get a feel for each period of life on the Cape in the reference section. It is actually because of Hannah that the Inn is here today. We were made aware of her presence and Laurie decided we had to save the Inn so Hannah had a place to stay.

I thought the bank would love that reason for the construction loan but we were approved anyway. The initial couple of hundred thousand did not go far and we made many repeat trips for assistance. Ellen Covell always came through for us.

Hannah opens doors and lights candles. She makes herself known through a cold blast of air from nowhere. It is as though she is seeking warmth and quite honestly is not a bad feeling. Laurie and our neighbor were the first to experience the feeling.

The doors were always open no matter how many times they were locked and checked. It is thought Hannah wants the doors to the Inn to remain open forever. We are trying to keep her happy. Laurie told me that no matter what "Don't piss off the ghost." I actually enjoy her presence but was kind of freaked out at first. I did get used to the annoyance of finding all the doors open every morning. I could not sleep one night and came to the Inn around 3AM. The front door had been triple bolted but was open wide. I went into the hidden room to get my tools but heard footsteps above. I went to get a flashlight thinking someone had found the door open and was looking around upstairs. Then I thought better as it may have been a break in and went to call the police. When I realized it may be Hannah entertaining friends I left the building until daylight.

The other two ghosts were named Fred and Paul. We were recently made aware of a fourth spirit that had committed suicide in the 50's. The water meter reader brought a copy of the death certificate of a German worker found in a bathroom. We were not familiar with that story but will try to put the pieces together. There were two other suicides of staff members by hanging. Paul was in the basement and Fred was in the Cupola. We still invite guests to visit the Cupola and see if Fred is hanging around.

We tell the guests to help themselves to any refreshments in the wait kitchen in the dining room. In the middle of the night Ed woke from his sleep on the sofa to what he thought was a female guest walking naked into the dining room. He said hello and she said hello and went back to sleep. He thought it was just another perk of being an Innkeeper. Several weeks later an employee was told by a family they had stopped in front of the Inn and looked up to see a naked lady dancing in the Belvedere. Ed knew there was no one on that level and realized it was not a guest he saw, but most likely it was Hannah.

Erin has heard voices of people talking including children when there was no one present. Megan has witnessed along with customers at the bar glasses traveling across a table as if being pushed. There is an entire chapter on the Inn found in the book *Haunted Cape Cod & The Islands,* by Mark Jasper. He and Jack Sheedy have given presentations at the Inn.

CHAPTER 9

GET OUT!

Don't they know we can't feed everyone in this town? Travelers had the only money available to spend and it had to stretch to make it possible to hold onto the Inn. The locals grew their own produce and traded for what they needed. The Inn was a target because food and shelter were a hot commodity. The banks failed and there was no value in the stock market. Suicides in New York on Wall Street were the talk of the country.

The rich with summer homes were not to be seen again. The locals saw many boarded up mansions and failed commercial properties. The Orleans Inn was still run as a boarding house and escaped the worst of the depression. From time to time it was used as a family home. The Inn did fall into some disrepair during the depression, and was in pretty bad shape by the early forties. Much of the business was in trade as no one trusted currency.

The Inn was still under the reputation from the party days and it became a pretty hard core drinking

Painting by Vernon Smith
1937

establishment. Food was basic and not very plentiful. Whiskey was plentiful and used quite liberally to wash away the fear of the time. Many boarders could not pay for their rooms and ended up working out the rent in trade.

The cold windy winters were only made worse by little fuel or coal to fire the furnace. The old boiler sat idle while the fireplaces provided the only warmth with locally cut firewood. The currency of the day became produce and wood. Fresh eggs and poultry were traded for a dinner or a few pennies.

The occasional automobile signaled a survivor from the depression and was admired by all. The roads were pretty much deserted and horses on the Cape were pressed into use again. The sailing ships were again used as an alternate mode of transportation.

As things started to improve some of the customs made necessary by the depression continued on the Cape. Much barter and trade continued in order to avoid taxes as well as the distrust in the banks. Art was becoming popular on the Cape and was often traded for room and board. The Cape provided a beautiful background for art and it flourished. Writers also flocked to the Cape for the peaceful serenity of the special peninsula.

Vernon Smith was one of the more famous artists on the Cape and he traded many of his paintings with local businesses. The Inn has obtained a copy of his painting of the Inn from 1936. It shows the beauty and color of the Inn from that period. The mansard roof and Cupola is a reddish slate with blue shutters on a white façade. Massive trees front Old County Road which at that time was the Old Kings Highway and the only road to Provincetown. The ground floor was actually open and we hear stories of children running under the Inn built on stilts. That level has been finished and hosts weddings.

The main level has a wrap around porch and seems very serene. The sign outside says only Orleans Inn. During future incarnations the Inn was known as The Orleans Inn of the Yankee Fisherman. At one time it was known as the Cove Inn and the Ellis Inn.

The lace curtains on the guest level are absolutely lovely. The ships knees under the mansard roof are beautiful. The walk around balcony no longer exists. It appears there is a delivery being made to the south entrance to the building which has been traditional since the Inn was built. There are power lines and utility poles with street lamps. The painting must have been made in the fall of 1936. The trees are turning a burnished gold and yellow. Young trees planted at the north end of the building would have to be removed for the future expansion of the dining room.

CHAPTER 10

BRUNO BURKHART

Vat in hell you think you are doing? Bruno yelled in his German accent to the contruction workers. The Burkharts were a strong willed German couple who saw something in the potential of the old Victorian structure on the waters of town Cove. Bruno wondered aloud of his decision to buy the funny looking building once known as Aaron's Folly.

He certainly was not a common sight especially so soon after the war. Many German-Americans fought to defend the country but the accent still made people nervous. The Inn was known as a local landmark and to be owned by a German was the scandal of the time. The French had made a significant presence during the transatlantic cable installation and operations. They were accepted by the English settlers on the Cape.

Today almost 50% of Americans have some connection to German heritage. The country almost chose German as the official language by the founding fathers. Germans were imported as settlers with strong backs and willing laborers. Many were used to build the railroads. Ed's ancestors worked with the railroad in Chicago. His mother is Irish and they were not readily accepted in this country especially in English New England.

Bruno hired a construction crew and almost broke their backs on the expansion of the Inn. He had a grandiose plan for the historic landmark which was all old world charm. He removed the north porch and built a massive two story addition attached to the building. The mansard roof was untouched and kept the character of the building. The ground floor enclosed the open stilt foundation and became the boiler and equipment room. The impressive dining room on the main level off the lobby was named the Brunella Room after Bruno and his wife. It was a very formal affair with elegant dining. Gentleman wore jackets and it became a special occasion place for celebrations.

The south side of the building was razed and the one story kitchen was replaced with a massive kitchen and guest rooms above. The ground floor was enclosed and used for storage. Again the mansard roof was saved and the Inn took on a blended look.

The most interesting addition was the east exposure addition. The main floor became the cabaret with French doors opening to a water level deck. The upper level became the aft deck lounge or today known as O'Hagan Irish Pub. This is the most popular room in the Inn and provides panoramic views of the Cove from all three walls. During snow storms it seems like you are inside one of the snow globes after being shaken. This room was actually falling off the building when Ed bought the Inn. The foundation gave way below and the ceiling had collapsed. The entire roof was raised by microlam cathedral beams and the room was opened with a cathedral ceiling. All the windows were replaced for a better view and reduced exposure to the elements. The entire room was gutted and a new mahogany full Victorian back bar was custom built with a huge horseshoe shaped bar.

The entire upper level was converted into a hotel with 14 rooms. Some of the rooms were of a very generous size and some were quite small. After Ed bought the Inn the small rooms were incorporated into adjoining rooms to create suites. The original layout had a long hallway with rooms on each side of the hall. This layout continues today with a very efficient design. The waterfront rooms are the even numbers and are the most popular especially in the busy summer season. Ed selected the numbering scheme for even numbers starting at the windmill on the water. It has worked well, however when someone is referring to a room from the past we have to go back and match up the numbers. For example room 4 is where some paranormal activity has taken place and people may refer to room 9 which is the number prior to our ownership. Room 5 is another interesting room. A book could be written on these two rooms alone.

The upper three levels remained untouched from the original 1875 construction and will remain that way with some minor redecorating and refurbishing.

Postcard of the Orleans Inn from the early 50's

CHAPTER 11

MOVIE STARS AND SINGERS

My son would love it here. The Sinatra's enjoyed one of the famous shows at the Orleans Inn and were referring to their son Frank. The quote is from the president of the Cape & Islands Tour Guide Association Dick Tellier. Dick shared this during the Annual Meeting of the combined Tour Directors and Concierge held each January at the Orleans Inn. Dick used to perform at the Inn and met the Sinatra's who were in the audience. Dick sang Old Cape Cod for the Group and he was amazing. Another memory of the Orleans Inn is made and will be recorded for posterity.

Rumors have Jennifer Anniston and Brad Pitt visiting the Inn but that could not be confirmed. I do remember talking briefly with a wonderful couple who could have been them but all I remember was how nice they were. Who knows? I'm clueless.

Elizabeth Taylor and Montgomery Cliff have been placed at the Inn as well. The Kennedy family is said to have used the Inn for private functions. None of the rumors can be confirmed as they have all been related from third parties. Obviously we cannot confirm nor deny any star sightings other than to say this was known as The Place on the Cape. It is interesting to see the Inn as the focal point of the community.

There are plans to bring back a celebration of Sinatra known as MY WAY. We hope this materializes especially in the light of the Sinatra connections. Several attempts to bring back the old dinner theater has seen mixed results. This will be a professional production with nightly performances by acclaimed singers.

The Inn was known for the Showmates. This was a musical revue and was perfected during the Costa ownership of the Inn. The family was extremely talented and thrilled generations with their performances. Heather sang as a child and was married here at the Inn 5/22/04. It was a very special celebration for a wonderful close knit family.

Ed had heard many stories of the Showmates and tried several times to bring in talent to produce the show. Times have changed and it was not possible to rely on paid talent. There is no substitute for family and the Costa family had an incredible production.

Both attempts to bring back the now infamous shows did not meet expectations. The Inn is after all a business and the highest and best business use is the core business.

The private receptions, restaurant and lodging are responsible for the resurrection of the Inn. The business plan will never stray far from the core business again.

The Showmates

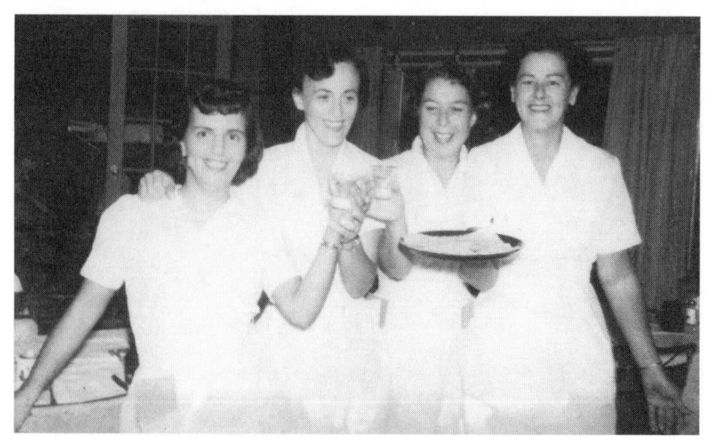

The Staff, 1950's

CHAPTER 12

THE SHOWMATES

The audience was roaring! The Showmates put on another rousing performance. Heather Costa was amazing in her vocal rendition. She had no idea that some twenty years later she would appear in a stunning gown and mesmerize another audience focused on her at an incredible wedding reception for 200 family members and guests. The only sad part was that Aunt Peggy was not present to celebrate. In spite of the Herculean efforts to save the family business Peggy Servidio succumbed to cancer the year earlier.

Peggy was known as the backbone of the Inn. Her husband Joe had overextended the Inn and drained the resources for off cape ventures at the Lakeside Inn. Peggy was left to try to salvage the Inn. The marriage ended in divorce and Peggy was left without a stake in the Inn. She did go to work at another restaurant but her heart and soul were at the Inn. She had visited Ryan and shared some information to help him. That was a very kind thing to do on her part.

The Showmates ended and the Inn contracted to essentially the bar part of the operations. Peggy was the core of the Inn but the losses were mounting. The Inn eventually was lost to foreclosure by the bank. The Inn was again vacant with an uncertain future.

The Inn was sold to the Sutphin family who tried unsuccessfully to operate the Inn. They did focus on getting the downstairs level functional and providing entertainment. The advertising for the Inn focused on entertainment and bands. The amount spent on advertising and entertainment was never recouped. By the time foreclosure came the Inn was in disrepair. The roof was leaking badly and serious damage had occurred.

The desperate attempts to hold on to the Inn left many bills unpaid as well as payroll and taxes not paid. By the time the Inn was padlocked, the sheriff had made several visits to the Inn arresting principals for bounced checks. Once was during the lunch hour and the word spread quickly the Inn was in trouble. By the time the newspapers were covering the story meals and sales taxes had not been paid and the building was padlocked.

After the Inn was unceremoniously auctioned to the highest bidder that deal fell through as the buyer did not have the cash required for the sale. The bank was becoming impatient and listed the property with American Heritage Realty. By the time Ed had purchased the property the Post Office was only too happy to give him the boxes of unpaid dunning notices to the old owners. Ed personally contacted each debtor and advised them of the change in ownership. Although Ed was not responsible for any of the bills he did offer the opportunity to provide services for the soon to be reopened Inn. Most of the vendors appreciated the opportunity and have been rewarded with nine years of loyalty by Ed and the Inn. The best decision Ed made was this expression of out-reach to vendors who had been burned by the prior owners. He felt if anyone deserved a crack at the business it was the creditors left holding the bag. They all have been richly rewarded. The bookkeeping service KaybeeTwo, was among those creditors. Ed called them first and met Jackie Keen. She has remained their bookkeeper since that date with only one slight interruption which was ill fated. Ed was told by the bank that he should try another service which had convinced them they were superior. That move almost cost the Maas family the ownership of the Inn and Ed fired the service and returned to Kaybee Two. Ed has remained loyal to this day. When Ed was overwhelmed by the enormity of debt, Bob Barker, Jackie's partner said it is like eating an elephant—one bite at a time. Well the elephant is almost gone but it has taken five years—one bite at a time.

When Ed was digging through the bills and reviewing the financial records left behind it was clear why they failed. They were spending money on advertising and entertainment.

He vowed that those two expenses would not jeopardize the finances of the Inn. Several times he strayed from that commitment and it had not been positive. Stick to the core and stay away from entertainment and advertising. That will prove successful in the long run. Word of mouth has proven to be the best advertising and marketing for the Orleans Inn.

One arrangement which was terminated was the tour boat operating from the inn. Ed met with the town administrator at the time and expressed concerns. The temporary permit for the dock was not going to be renewed. The Captain had a reputation for drinking and ran over a kayacker. The town had concerns about the operation and asked our assistance. Ed found out the Captain was involved in a major drug bust which made him unpopular. Supposedly a major shipment was planned to be offloaded to many small boats off the Nauset inlet. The captain went drinking and was bragging about all the money he was going to make. The authorities got word and arrested quite a few boaters involved. Ed told the owner of the boat he would not renew the lease. The town now allows a commercial sightseeing boat to operate from the town dock without charge and provides free storage over the winter. It hardly seems fair to the other tour operator.

CHAPTER 13

ABANDONMENT AND FORECLOSURE

The newspaper accounts were merciless. For at least the second time in just a few years the Inn was in foreclosure again. The current owners did not have the wherewithal to survive another winter and lost the Inn in November. The auction drew only a few qualified bidders. The Inn was unceremoniously auctioned for $410,000.

While reading the Cape Codder account of the auction Ed exclaimed, Oh my God, if I had known I would have bid on it!" Laurie asked what I was talking about while having coffee looking out on the lake of our Weston, Fl home. I was connecting with our beloved Cape Cod vicariously through the Cape Codder newspaper.

Neither Laurie nor I had ever been in the Orleans Inn but had both passed it thousands of times in the past. It was really run down and Ed had often commented that it needed a paint job. Ed remembers one time over the past 25 years wondering what was going on inside the funny looking building. He remembers walking tentatively up the ramp and noticing the photographs of the entertainers posted on the wall. He somehow felt uncomfortable and peeked through the door. He did not feel right and could not bring himself to go inside. He left not thinking about it again until reading the news article.

Ed put down the newspaper not dwelling on what might have been. He went about his routine of spending time with his children and preparing for the Confirmation classes he taught for ten years. He had a thriving healthcare consulting business and was consumed with the clients needs seven days a week. He loved his job as a hospital administrator but that was stolen from him by the Columbia acquisition of Galen Healthcare. Six weeks of hell ensued until the final day of working for the greedy monopolistic corporation. Ed refused to blindly follow their directions to violate the law and was concerned that he could not risk going to jail for their corrupt directives. He saw the demise of class and honor exhibited by David Jones and Jack Clark prior to the disgusting tactics of Columbia.

On Friday Ed received the Top Performer award and a six figure bonus. On Saturday he received the Hospital Administrator of the Year Award by the Palm Beach County Medical Society. On Monday, the new director of the region for Columbia heard about the award and proceeded directly to the hospital to fire Ed. The only reason given was she wanted her own person. Yeah, one that would conspire with her questionable tactics. Ed had already anticipated the action and was actually relieved. He went straight to his best friend and attorney Howard Furman. Ed gave Howard the change of control agreement and set up the Maas Group, Inc. Healthcare Consulting that day.

Laurie and the children were devastated. Ed tried to reassure them and threw himself into the new venture. His first client came as a referral from his dear friend Byron Mathews a prominent healthcare attorney and took on Columbia in a Certificate of Need battle. It was the perfect opportunity for Ed to deal with the hurt and humiliation dealt by them.

Ed started receiving overtures from Columbia and had a cease and desist letter from Howard sent to them. There was no way he would ever work for that organization again. He began a crusade of not for profit hospitals to protect themselves against the aggressive takeover tactics of Columbia. Unfortunately some of the CEO's were cutting their own deals in selling out their hospitals to the enemy. It made him sick.

Ed began working with more diverse groups including physician IPA's. He enjoyed the thrill of representing thousands of physicians in negotiating against major HMO's. One particular group offered Ed millions in stock to sell out the physician group. Ed declined and they told him he was crazy. That particular company is bankrupt and the stock is worthless. The physician group was not Ed's to sell and he would not sell them out. This actually occurred at the time Ed was purchasing the Inn. It was a real temptation but Ed told them in no uncertain terms and some quite colorful language where to shove their rich offer. He had no idea what he would use to purchase the Inn but it all worked out.

Ed took the biggest risk of his life and somehow it all fell into place with help from friends and family. The risk paid off and the Inn will hopefully remain in the Maas family for generations to come. Ed feels it was meant to be and was a divine providence.

Ed tried to assist Ryan in any way possible. He was upset when the Inn lost money operationally the first winter. Ryan had a function scheduled and had become late in paying the bills. Ed was tapped out and was falling behind as well. The electricity was turned off the morning of the scheduled function. Ryan went to Mike at Goose Hummock and was distraught. Mike asked what was wrong as Ryan was pale and scared. Mike wrote him a check on the spot and the function went on without a hitch. We will never forget his kindness and have learned to put money aside in the summer for the lean winter months. It is nice to have such a goodhearted neighbor as Mike and Goose Hummock.

Ed has tried to be a good neighbor to the town as it owns the Windmill Park on one side and the Town

Landing on the other. There have been concerns over the boat storage and repairs on Town Landing during the winter and spring. It is hoped the town will prevent these activities from happening in the future.

Ed has offered easements to the town and granted a license to gain access to the Windmill Park. The town had the property and installed the windmill but had no way to access the park. Ed donated the right to build an access and make the Park accessible to everyone.

Town Cove—Orleans, MA
Painting by Kathy Kleekamp, 2005

A note from the artist . . .

The charming seaside town of Orleans, MA on the elbow of Cape Cod was first settled in 1642 by Nicholas Snow and his family. The colonial economy depended on commercial fishing and agriculture, especially the growing of corn and wheat. Generations later, Aaron Snow built his home on Town Cove to be next to his schooner which transported goods from all over New England to the Snow Family Store which operated out of the home.

Today, the enlarged and lovingly restored home is known as The Orleans Inn. Run by Ed and Laurie Maas, visitors to the inn can easily "step back in time" and enjoy the beauty and rich heritage of the Orleans area. The Jonathan Young windmill, first built in the town about 1720 was moved to Hyannisport in 1897. Returned to the Orleans Historical Society in 1983, it was brought to Town Cove Park, where it now stands.

This is an imaginary scene incorporating some modern changes with that long ago more simple and charming way of life. This is a limited edition print from my original oil painting. I hope you enjoy it.

—Kathryn Kleekamp
PO Box 1300, Sandwich MA 02563 • 508.833.1271
kleekamp@adelphia.net • www.SandwichArt.com

CHAPTER 14

ARTISTS

"Mr. Maas, this is Kathy Kleekamp in Sandwich. You don't know me but I did an oil painting of the Town Cove featuring the Orleans Inn. Bob Tucker suggested that you might be interested in carrying prints in your gift shop." Ed hesitated and said that it was a coincidence that he and Megan were on their way to Sandwich for a Cape&Islands Concierge meeting and that he would stop in to meet her.

Within a few hours Ed was viewing one of the most beautiful paintings he had ever seen. Megan was awestruck. Kathy was a very pleasant and talented artist who graciously invited them into her home. Ed immediately made an offer for the original and wanted to purchase 100 of the limited edition prints for gifts. Kathy promised to get back to them with her decision.

Ed and Megan proceeded with a print to the meeting at the Sandwich Glass museum and everyone was impressed. The Inn was captured in a Victorian setting with hotel guests disembarking from a horse drawn stage coach and picnicking on the lawn of the Windmill.

After the meeting Ed and Megan could not wait to show the print to Josh and Erin. It is now at the entrance of the Inn and inspired the theme of the 130th anniversary celebration. Plans were made for 5/15/05 to have a Victorian picnic at the Inn and invite participants to dress in Victorian garb with horse drawn carriages.

The Barnstable Patriot was contacted to consider the painting as their cover for the Town of Orleans information book. The prints will be available for sale at the Inn signed and numbered limited to 250.

The original is now hanging in the entrance of the Inn and draws rave reviews. It is nice to have a vivid reminder of the rich history of the Inn. It joins original works by Jack Kitson, Karen North Wells, Arthur Long and Clifford Gustafson. Original art is one of the best investments that can be made and the extra benefit is they can be enjoyed every day. The feel they give to the Inn is amazing. Guests are invited to tour the gallery any time and enjoy the beauty each artist gave to the paintings.

A gifted rendering of the Inn
from Architectural Design Incorporated, Christmas 1997

The Maas Family
Christmas at the Inn, 2004
Shannon and Javier Lirio—married at the Inn 2003, expecting their first child 2005, Meagan, Caitlin, Logan, Shawn, Erin, Ryan, Ed and Laurie

CHAPTER 15

MAAS PRESS CONFERENCE

Sitting in the dining room which was looking pretty shabby the reporters asked questions as to the plans for the Orleans Inn. I did not know and honestly answered that if nothing else it would be a large home for our family. Every decision since that time has been to create a homelike feeling at the Inn. Laurie and the children saw to that happening.

The reporter for the Cape Codder, Suzanna Graham-Pye said she had written the history of the Inn for the menu when she worked for a private public relations firm. We have not changed it except to update it and it really says it all. We have reprinted it in this book.

The reporter from the Cape Cod Times, Susan Milton asked to take a picture in front of the Orleans Inn sign. We did and it was carried in the next day edition. OK the word is out. Hopefully the rumors will stop and the truth will be known. It is interesting that to date there are still misconceptions and we constantly try to get the facts straight. For some reason I have to repeatedly correct rumors that I am from New Jersey. I don't know where that came from and I don't mind it but the only thing I know about it is the Jersey Turnpike that I take on my trips back and forth to Florida. Some times I almost don't feel like correcting them.

The floodgates opened when word got out there was fresh meat and there was a feeding frenzy. It was merciless and relentless. I wish I knew then what I know now and would have been much more protective. It is hard to sort out those trying to help from the throngs looking to get their hand in your pocket. I tell the children to be careful of the non customers as they have another agenda. Our business is the focus on our customers and to protect ourselves against all others. It is amazing we survived the onslaught.

I have heard derogatory comments that I am a 'Washashore'. I correct them and state emphatically that I am a Cracker from Florida. I don't know what the obsession is about the Washashore vs Local thing but it is silly. There really is no definition between the two and it is terrible to pigeonhole people. We try to stay away from the classifications and treat everyone the same. We try to treat everyone as we would treat our family.

We did find the wrong contractors and narrowly avoided losing everything as a result. When contractors tell you they are licensed and insured don't accept their word alone. We learned the hard way that the charm and assurances are not to be believed. We had to replace a majority of the work done by the original contractor. The plumbers had to be replaced. The electrical contractor fired the only person who knew what he was doing and we had to bring him in to sort things out after we opened. The new roof leaked worse than the old one and had to be torn off and replaced by a legitimate contractor. The emergency pumps out side were never remounted and cost a fortune to repair the damage. The signage was never replaced after being removed to re-side and now can not be used.

We were too far along to turn back and eventually fired all the contractors and finished the job ourselves. Ryan and I spent many sleepless nights working around the clock. We barely made the drop dead date in surviving the contractors. There are legitimate contractors on the Cape. I just did not find them. I now know who they are and am happy to give recommendations. We help other businesses and residents in any way possible. We also have emergency equipment which we share whenever asked. We are probably the only business that maintains spare Buss fuses at $120 apiece but we always know they are available for us or others to use. A business can be shut down without them and several are needed at a moments notice when the power goes down. We have the equivalent of a hardware store in the workshop to address any emergency. Minor electrical, plumbing and carpentry are essential training for operating the Inn.

Shawn teaches high school drama and literature. He bartends in the summer. Shannon teaches forth grade and mentors other teachers in Florida. Ryan helps with projects at the Inn when not training managers. Megan helps with PR and marketing. Erin met Josh at Johnson and Wales. Josh is just like family and is general manager. Erin and Megan are the first twins to obtain MBA's at Johnson and Wales. Brandon is pursuing his education. Caitlin is studying for college. Logan is involved in everything. The family works together as a team to provide a wonderful guest experience.

CHAPTER 16

MEMORIES

Watching the guests' reactions as they step through the door is gratifying. Whether they are remembering earlier visits to the inn or the first visit triggering distant pleasant memories of the past, the guests all seem to stop in their tracks commenting to give them a minute to take in things. We were so anxious to give the community a peak at the Inn we had a sneak preview in March prior to opening in May. The town of Orleans celebrated its bicentennial in 1997. The town had a concert for Beethoven music from the period and we hosted a complimentary reception after the concert.

We had just finished cleaning up after the contractors and it was amazing we were able to pull it off. We had a one day permit from the health department and a temporary permit to use the building for the event. It was a good dry run. Our friend John Sherman arrived first as we were just starting to prepare the food. I told him I was going to go home and take a shower and he laughed. There are 200 people behind me. You aren't going anywhere. Thank God I listened to him and told Laurie the same. We were both in our cleaning clothes and started preparing the food in the wait kitchen. As soon as we could bring it out it disappeared. In an hour it was all over and Laurie and I looked at each other wondering what had just happened. The guests had come in and piled coats on the floor with a mountain forming in no time. There was no furniture. The guests just wanted to know that the Inn was all right and would be reopened. It was quiet again.

We received another temporary one day permit and alcohol license for a wedding. The guests had a wonderful time and we were not paid the balance. It was a real blow to our finances and despite several letters which were ignored we never received payment.

We finally got a temporary partial Certificate of Occupancy and were in business May 15, 1997. We opened the Inn by stages and opened the function room in July and the lodging level in August. We missed the majority of the season and that hurt the finances as well.

The mission statement was posted at the front entrance and says it all. The Mission of the Orleans Inn is to provide comfort, food, service and lodging for a lifetime of memories and friendship. We make sure staff is familiar with the mission and carry it out daily.

Most guests have some connection to the Inn in the past. Some have had multi generational experience at the Inn. It is nice to see grandmothers bring granddaughters telling them their grandmothers brought them to the Inn as children.

Many memories are created and relived at the Inn. Whether it is a wedding, funeral, birthday, anniversary, baby shower or Christening, the Inn is the perfect setting.

The reactions of guests are gratifying and make it all worthwhile. So often we hear guest walk in and say "Let me just take it all in". We love to have them take their time and enjoy all the decorations. So many say it is like stepping back in time. There was a much more relaxed pace and we try to recreate that feeling. The panoramic views of the Cove are breathtaking. Whether it is a bright sunshine day or the glittering moonlight off the Cove it seems like a million diamonds glittering on the water.

We love the comments that guests write in the guest book. Some of our favorites are:

Had a great dinner with family-looking for a permanent home on the Cape to have many repeats!

Thank you for a fantastic time!

We had no idea what to expect before we arrived, but

the Orleans Inn is better than we could have possibly imagined! The most wonderful view from the deck and the beautiful rooms as well make it a fabulous place to stay! Thank you for a memorable (short) stay here in Orleans.

Thank you for feeding us such wonderful food at such a late hour. I'll mention you in my book.

Thanks for a perfect evening: food, water, cheer. What more could we ask for?

Had a great desert & coffee in your quaint Inn. Thanks for staying open and putting up with our laughter.

Great to be back in Old Cape Cod.

A lovely place to find oneself.

Thank you for making our second anniversary so special! We had a wonderful time.

This has been an enjoyable visit.

Thank you for great food and a very enjoyable evening.

The dinner was wonderful and I enjoyed seeing your lovely place.

Great lunch, Great service, Thanks to Megan, lovely place.

Thank you for your warmth and hospitality and for being so generous.

With gratitude for a wonderful stay and with great pleasure & reminiscence of John Steinbeck.

Like coming home. Thank you.

Wonderful esperience.

Superb Lobster Salad.

Thanks for pampering us. The inn is great, The food delicious, but the best is your family. Best of luck to you all.

Great oysters!

What a wonderful place to visit!

Great martinis!

We so love the Orleans Inn. We have brought numerous family & friends

We're having a wonderful time.

We love this place—moving back to CT but will be back to visit this lovely place.

Enjoyed it & would love to come back!

Great service & excellent view! Be back soon!

Very pleasant atmosphere and service.

Pet and people friendly-hope to see you soon.

What a wonderful place who is accepting of our family pet friends too!

What a lovely setting.

Wonderful meal, delightful view & very friendly staff.

Wonderful dinner indeed! I'll be back!

Thanks for making our stay so special!

CHAPTER 17

AN INN WITH A MESSAGE

Whether it is the ten commandments framed on the wall or the poignant messages found throughout the Inn, it is clear that the Inn provides a respite for the guests as they take in the beauty of the inn. The sayings on the wall are very special and have deep meaning or whimsical phrases. There are also special awards and photographs as well as family art.

There are special messages through out and have meaning for just about everyone. The most popular is:

THINGS WE CAN LEARN from a DOG

Never pass up the opportunity to go for a joy ride.

Allow the experience of fresh air and the wind in your face to be pure ecstasy.

When loved ones come home, always run to great them.

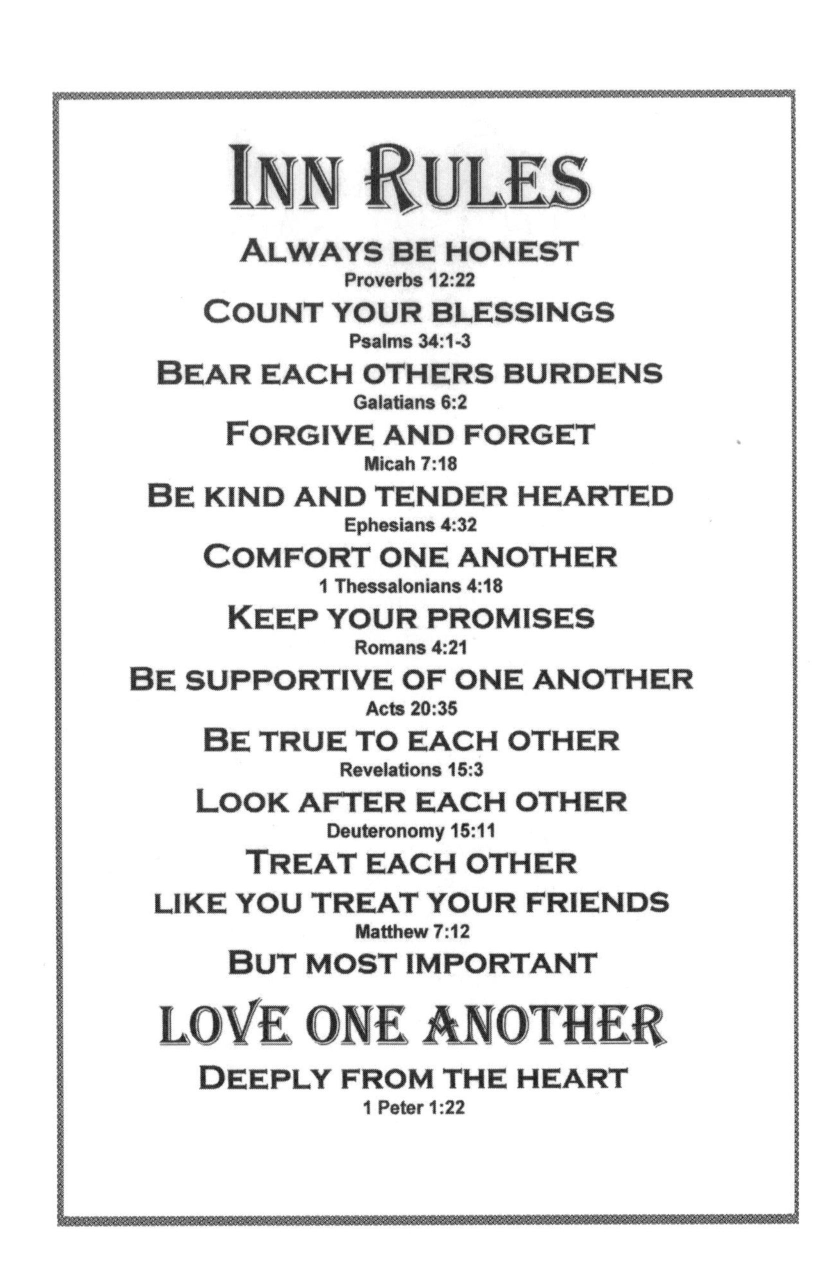
INN RULES
ALWAYS BE HONEST
Proverbs 12:22
COUNT YOUR BLESSINGS
Psalms 34:1-3
BEAR EACH OTHERS BURDENS
Galatians 6:2
FORGIVE AND FORGET
Micah 7:18
BE KIND AND TENDER HEARTED
Ephesians 4:32
COMFORT ONE ANOTHER
1 Thessalonians 4:18
KEEP YOUR PROMISES
Romans 4:21
BE SUPPORTIVE OF ONE ANOTHER
Acts 20:35
BE TRUE TO EACH OTHER
Revelations 15:3
LOOK AFTER EACH OTHER
Deuteronomy 15:11
TREAT EACH OTHER
LIKE YOU TREAT YOUR FRIENDS
Matthew 7:12
BUT MOST IMPORTANT
LOVE ONE ANOTHER
DEEPLY FROM THE HEART
1 Peter 1:22

When it's in your best interest, practice obedience.

Let others know when they've invaded your territory.

Take naps and stretch before rising.

Run, romp and play daily.

Eat with gusto and enthusiasm.

Be loyal.

Never pretend to be something you're not.

If what you want lies buried, dig for it.

When someone is having a bad day, be silent, sit close by and nuzzle them gently.

Thrive on attention and let people hug you.

Avoid biting when a simple growl will do.

On hot days, drink lots of water and lay under a shady tree.

When you're happy, dance around and wag your entire body.

No matter how often you're scolded, don't buy into the guilt thing and pout-run right back and make friends.

Delight in the simple joy of a long walk.

Another favorite is the Senility Prayer:

Grant me the serenity to forget the people I never liked,

The good fortune to run into the people I do like,

The eyesight to know the difference.

For those dealing with loss:

When someone you know becomes a memory
The memory becomes a treasure

The most often requested copy of a prayer is:

Dear God,
So far today, I've done all right.
I haven't gossiped and I haven't lost my temper.
I haven't been grumpy, nasty or selfish
And I am glad of that!
But in a few minutes, God,
I'm going to get out of bed and from then on,
I'm probably going to need a lot of help.
Thank you!
Amen

CHAPTER 18

OUR GUESTS

Michele and Max are amazing. Foochie is their most beautiful Chinese Fu dog. He is like a child. Ed was speaking with Max one day about his favorite author and Max said he knew John Steinbeck personally. Steinbach had such an impression on Ed growing up. Ed was a ninth grade student at Redland Junior High School. He has spent eight years at Sacred Heart Catholic School in Homestead and was yearning for the freedom of public School. His older sister Carol went into the convent after 12 years of parochial school. His older brother went in to the seminary for high school and college. Ed was concerned about the private tuition costs and wanted to ease the burden on his parents. They were disappointed with his decision at first but were reassured when he did well. He was so determined to do well and continue in pubic school that he forged his first interim report that he was failing algebra. He struggled to bring the grade up and his parents were never aware of the difficulty. He had a homeroom teacher Mr. Cokyl, who was a friend of the family and encouraged him to succeed. His English teacher Mrs. Barrows took the effort to have Ed transferred to Honors English as a challenge. The mixed feelings of leaving a favorite teacher and the fear of the competition of the smartest students spurred Ed to exceed. He took all honors classes in high school as a result. He would go to the library and check out books that were of interest and challenging. He selected Grapes of Wrath because it was the thickest not knowing of the incredible impact Steinbeck would have on his life. He then read every one of Steinbeck's works. What an honor to have met Max who knew the author personally. He cherishes the gift from Max and Michele from the Harvard Bookstore.

Marty and Laura Paul are another amazing couple. Many thousands of guests stop in to dine at the Inn and some of them return to stay overnight as guests. This was the case with Marty and Laura. Laura fell in love with the Christmas decorations especially the shadow box Waltzers. She asked Marty to bring her back to see them and now visits several times a season. Marty is an incredible photographer and has given us a picture of the Cove in winter. The fishing boat is covered in snow and is a striking contrast.

The Bradburies came to us out of default. Their reservation was at a motel in town which was musty and very disappointing. They checked out and came to stay with us. They have returned every year and we have watched Kelsey grow into a beautiful young woman. Judy is a children's book author and is extremely talented. She has given autographed books to Shannon for her classroom. Gene is a great guy and the family is special.

Many families think of the Inn as their beach home and return time after time. We now have dates that are booked two years in advance to make sure they have that special time on the Cape. We have always had a no cancellation penalty and know that things do come up and plans change. We have never kept a deposit and encourage reservations as far in advance as possible as they can always be changed or released. We get to know the families and they become like family to us. The book Open for the Season gives a great feel for this type of Inn operation and is available in the library of the Orleans Inn. Ryan had an assignment to read it in college Hospitality Management. He gave it to Ed who devoured it. It is the single best read on hospitality ever written. Erin found an original copy for Ed's birthday which is worth a small fortune. He cherishes it in his library.

Suite 2 has had very special guests who have recorded memories of their stay. The following is a sample of the notes they have left in the guest book:

This room is warm, comfortable & provided much needed rest & escape.

We enjoyed seeing the sun rise from behind the hills. Also, we should have brought binoculars to watch the flock of ducks diving for food. Enjoy the holidays. God bless you as we celebrate the birth of our Lord and Savior Jesus Christ.

Our room was warm & so comfortable. The food last night was perfect as well as everyone here. Thank you for a wonderful stay with friendly gracious people.

We're going to always remember our stay. Genuine New England hospitality! Wonderful seafoods from our shores, prepared perfect. A very restful stay. We thank you very much. We'll see you soon. God Bless our great land.

In a world that is filled with cold, its nice to know that there still exists warmth and caring. This is such a place! Thank you for making our stay (anniversary) that much more enjoyable. We love being by the Ocean and come every chance we get!! We travel a bit to see light-houses and in all of our stays at different places we think that Orleans Inn is one of the nicest places we've stayed. God Bless You!

As our third visit to the Orleans Inn draws to a close, we leave with the same comfortable memories of past visits genuinely relaxed atmosphere, warm surroundings and enjoyable and friendly innkeeper and staff. The seal that frolicked in the waters outside our room yesterday was an added treat to our wonderful stay. We will return and I suspect he will as well! So, thank you again for an enjoyable stay.

We came on a sad mission: to bring our father-in-law Arthur Franklin Croft, a 20 year + resident of Eastham, back home to his final resting place. The beautiful view from our windows was comforting, and we were quite touched by the thoughtfulness and generosity of our host and his staff. Most of our memories of the Cape are wonderful, and the pain of this one has been eased by the kindness and beauty we have experienced at the Orleans Inn.

From North Carolina to Cape Cod I have come over the last two weeks to work with a local bank. The weather has been cold, the work has been hard, the Orleans Inn has been a blessing. The warmth and generosity of Ed and his staff have truly made this a place to come home to each night.

A comfy cozy retreat from a very rainy drive. Waking to a starlit nite and sun shiny morn. Happy Birthday to me.

What a fantastic view of the Town Cove from Room 2! Seeing the loons dive under the water for such long periods of time is fascinating. The sunrise is unsurpassed as is your lobster bisque soup. Megan & Erin are such lovely girls & very helpful. (Our twin granddaughters enjoyed meeting them last summer.) You have made the Orleans Inn into a lovely, comfortable place. We love it.

Beautiful view, wonderful hospitality! A much needed rest before work in Worcester, MA. The flowers all over the Cape are beautiful! Truly treasured moments at the Orleans Inn.

After having a reunion with another family on the Cape—and having our family's annual "Birthday Bash" we found it a great comfort to return to the Inn each night. We enjoyed ourselves immensely and will probably return.

How wonderful to hear the welcoming "Hi! It's so good to have you back" from Ed! Our second visit to the Orleans Inn is still a special placewarm and friendly and clean. Ed and his staff truly make their guests feel comfortable—a home away from home. And, the dining room menu was delicious with the added pleasure of a young, gifted 15 year-old pianist. All the best, we look forward to our next visit.

We enjoyed every minute of our "getaway" to Cape Cod right before the school year begins! It was a special trip for us since it may be one of our last vacations alone together—as I am 8 weeks pregnant! We went to Nauset Beach, Fort Hill, Provincetown and to many great restaurants. We loved the view from our room! It was cool and overcast during our four days here, but it was a nice break from the summer heat. We can't wait to come back again—maybe next time with a little boy or girl.

Since our arrival on Friday evening God has given us a beautiful weekend and this lovely place. Our daughter's wedding took place in the park near the windmill under sunny skies with the scenic view of boats in the harbor behind us. It couldn't have been more picturesque!!! Our stay here was truly memorable...

As we pack up to head back home to our regular daily routines, we realize how lucky and fortunate we are to have spent the past 3 days in "Paradise". We were treated with respect and genuine friendship by Ed and his staff and were catered to every step of the way. We were treated like family and made to feel as though the Orleans Inn was not just a place to stay but was our home. We wish Ed and his family the very best in life and we shall return.

We came here for Dave & Vicki Groo's wedding. My family and I didn't know what to expect. The weather couldn't have been nicer. This is our first trip to the Cape. Thank you for a wonderful stay. We hope to come again some day.

We had a comfortable, quiet weekend here—leaving our 3 children home with grandparents. The food was great, the atmosphere was wonderful even if we had a weekend of record cold weather. We hope to make this an annual event.

We woke up to a beautiful day! Thanks for letting us use the bed-

Thanks for another great visit. We enjoy your hospitality & the food is delicious. This visit was as comfortable as the weekend of the wedding when our crew took over the entire Inn. Thanks again.

~

We enjoyed spending our anniversary here. We had a wonderful time this weekend. It is nice to see a family owned business can still prosper in America. Good Luck with the Inn.

~

What a warm, snug retreat on a cold, blustery November evening. Your beautiful Inn provided us with a well needed respite. We enjoyed waking to the brilliant sunshine flooding the room. Kudos to the chef. We had an excellent meal. Thank you for your sincere hospitality. We hope you and your family have a wonderful holiday season.

~

First & Foremost, Happy Birthday to the Inn's owner Ed Maas, today on your Half Century Celebration! Have a wonderful, healthy, prosperous next 50. We chose this picture to write alongside because of the warmth and hospitable reception we were welcomed with. Also, the comfort we experienced, Just Like Home! It was a magnificent weekend, good weather, great food, greater family fun. We can only "Dream" of a speedy return and hope others find as much as we did here at “The INN”. With love and respect and admiration! Your brother Fritz, Tracey and Kids! God Bless America

The easiest way to compliment you all is first to say “THANK YOU”.

Day after Funny Cide’s win at the Preakness in Maryland...

We enjoyed ourselves— a little biking
a little snacking
a little tanning
(a little snoring)

and a wonderful time.
– The Three Sisters

A wonderful stay although short. Thanks for all the tips on what to see. We can’t wait to return and see more! Dinner was delicious too!

Two weary British Tourists. Enjoyed the quiet, the comfort and the view. Many Thanks.

We have very much enjoyed our stay!! And feel lucky to have found the Orleans Inn. Everything was great from the accommodations to the food all provided with super service. Thank you so much for making our first stay on the Cape so wonderful and memorable! We will make every effort to return as soon as possible. Ps. the lobster bisque was amazing!!!

Dear Ed Maas and family and Staff, Thank you!!! For making us feel so welcome here. Your friendliness, hospitality, and genuine kindness is so refreshing to find. Thank you!! We will be back, many times! Kindest regards.

Our world was upside down, but it got perfectly clear as there wasn't anything to fear, for all of our roads lead to know where. To what lies ahead of US, was our destination...Our destination is still ahead of US...This was just one more stop in between...and this stop was quite memorable...

Our stay with you here at the Inn has been wonderful and so relaxing—memory making at it's best. We love your family atmosphere. The kindness shown to us by you and your staff have been second to none. We can only hope to come back and visit you sometime in the future. May God's richest blessings be graciously and generously poured out upon you and your family!

A glorious wedding day for my son Jonathon Sgro and his bride Gwendolyn Schneider—2:30 pm at the Jonathon Young Windmill and a unique reception Party—relaxed setting... the Town Cove lively with Sailboats. Among the special guests were Jon's brothers Kenneth & Daniel Sgro. The chosen menu was prepared perfectly. So, thank you Ed and family.

Thank you for a special nite in RM #2. Enjoyed your hospitality and the wonderful view from the window. Your Inn has made a wonderful memory for us on our first trip to Cape Cod.

Ed Maas & Family, the Cape is a very special place to us. We enjoy the winter her & the beauty of the season. The 16" of snow this latest Nor'easter dumped was a special treat. Most of all the excellent food, service & hospitality we've found here at the Orleans Inn is yet to be beat. This was our second stay and we were very pleased. We are looking forward to many more. You made us feel like part of your family. This is the perfect place to disconnect from the "rat race" and relax. Even our Westie "Lily" feels at home here and says a woof of Thanks. We're looking forward to our next visit. Wishing you & your family the very best!

Dear Ed and family, It is so nice to have your comfortable inn to provide our home away-from-home. (The plumber & electrician will be repairing our house for the next few weeks.) What a beautiful suite—both sunsets & sunrises!

To Ed & Staff, Enjoyed your hospitality Immensely! Next trip to Cape will be spent at the Orleans Inn.

ONLY IN ORLEANS
ROCK HARBOR
IMAGE FROM PHOTO BY KIM ROBB
ORLEANS · CAPE COD
CHAMBER OF COMMERCE INC.
ED MAAS
THE ORLEANS INN
COMMUNITY SERVICE AWARD
FEBRUARY 2002

COMMUNITY SUPPORT

Ed has parents that made their children believe they could do anything. This is an amazing fact because seven children were a strain on the salary Dad made working for the State of Florida Agricultural Research Station. Mom did not work outside of the house until the youngest started kindergarten. The small amount of money went first to the church and parochial school tuition. They set values which have stayed with us all.

Ed's Aunts, Uncles and Grandmothers all stressed education and work ethic. His sister and brothers were genius level intelligence. We did not want anything because we felt rich with each other. We thought we had the best family and did not think about material things. We worked in the fields to supplement the family income and all contributed.

We were taught self confidence and the importance of faith. We went to Mass as a family and were all required to put our 10 cent allowance into the collection basket. It was good training on how to share and contribute to society. We felt it was an honor to help others and always looked for the opportunity. The boys all served as altar boys and the girls helped in the convent. We were always the first to volunteer to help in any way.

Ed's cousin Mary Ann was as close as a sister to him. They were almost like twins as they were about a week apart in age. Her parents were very good to Ed and enclosed is a picture of the First Communion at Sacred Heart. Mary Ann dedicated her life to helping others and is very special. Her mother, Aunt Joan is a very kind and giving person. Her father, Larry helped Ed's family and was an inspiration to Ed. He convinced Ed to start investing in mutual funds when he was 12 years old. It was this type of advice that made it possible for Ed to survive in business. Uncle Larry led Eddie to believe anything was possible. He is truly missed and would have loved to have seen the Inn.

The teachers at Sacred Heart fostered a confidence and sense of commitment like no other. We were in the choir and toured often. We gave public speeches and did readings at church. We were well prepared for high school and college. The working world was also a breeze as we were taught the strong sense of ethics. Ed began a career in hospitals starting at the bottom and becoming a nationally and internationally recognized expert.

Walter Loebenberg took an interest in Ed and gave him every opportunity to succeed. Bernadine Braithwaite was the chief of operations for Walter and taught Ed well. She taught him the importance of community involvement and the sense of responsibility. Walter was like a second father to Ed. Walter is one of six people that influenced Ed the most. They are all Jewish. Walter started a Holocaust Museum in Florida. Gary Arenson also helped Ed financially and professionally as well as being a close friend. Phil Rosenthal and Brad Feuer as well as Howard Furman were all mentors to Ed. Maurice Lewitt was a strong influence on Ed and assisted him greatly. Ed will never forget them.

Ed was encouraged to become involved in the Chamber of Commerce. He has become President of five separate Chambers and founded one in a new area. Ed's greatest pride is being elected president of the Orleans Chamber of Commerce.

Ed was asked several years ago to assist the Cape & Islands Concierge Association. It has been a wonderful experience. He has served on its board since the first year of organization and is very proud of its service. The mutual benefit has assisted the Inn.

Ed was honored to be elected to the board of the Cape & Islands United Way. Richard Brothers does an amazing job with that organization and the impact on the community is phenomenal. Richard is hard to say no to and has the greatest board of directors around.

The Inn will continue to support the United Way on an ongoing annual commitment.

The Orleans Inn supports the community through contributions and in kind support in the area of $100,000 per year. The first 10 percent of revenues are dedicated to charitable contributions. This is a tithing philosophy which continues as a commitment of the Inn.

1959 First Communion
Ed and cousin Mary Ann

CHAPTER 20

RECEPTIONS

The greatest satisfaction of owning the Inn is witnessing the wonderful special occasions that take place year round. Whether it is a wedding, anniversary, birthday or christening the Inn is the perfect venue. We love to see families get together. Special occasions take precedence over everything else at the Inn.

The following are sample letters over the past few years the Maas family has received:

Dear Ed,

Once again the Historical Society wishes to thank you for the generous support you rendered by hosting the luncheon. The perfect day allowed the touring group to fully appreciate the dramatic location the Orleans Inn has on Town Cove.

Dear Mr. Maas:

My family and I want to sincerely thank you and your family for all that you did helping us celebrate our daughter Patricia's marriage to Sean yesterday. The reception was extraordinary. The food was excellent. I think that the scallop recipe is an absolute winner. Your family and staff went out of their way to provide excellent service and even were nice enough to do little extras such as helping us keep track of gift envelopes and give special accommodations to some of our guests. The setting of your Inn on Town Cove only added more charm to the occasion. The Town of Orleans is fortunate indeed to have such a well managed, quality establishment.

Ed Maas & family,

Thank you again for making our wedding day flow smoothly when we needed the help! Thank you for being so kind & thoughtful with our family staying at your Inn.

Dear Ed,

Just want to thank you & your staff for making our wedding reception so perfect! Everyone had an incredible time and the food was SO delicious. Your business is a model of friendliness and professionalism. We'll be back for our 25th wedding anniversary.

Wow!!! Thank-you for all your hard work. You were wonderful to work with and the day was just fantastic. Everything was perfect from the linens to the food. Again, thank-you for every last thing.

Dear Ed, Josh and the whole crew at the Orleans Inn,

A belated yet heartfelt thank you for a marvelous wedding reception at the Inn. It was an absoulutely fantastic evening. We just wanted to once again heap praise and thanks upon all involved in the organizing and running of the reception. The food was excellent—scrumptious and plentiful, the service wonderful—efficient and unobtrusive. The day proved perfect for the use of the deck and watching the sun go down whilst having dinner was an extra romantic touch that far exceeded our expectations. All our family and friends are still commenting on how wonderful the whole evening was. Once again we thank you for helping to make our special day the memorable event that it was.

What a Perfect Day! Everyone had a fabulous time, the food was wonderful & the atmosphere couldn't have been any greater! Thanks again to all of you at the Orleans Inn, who made the occasion for Seth & Tara so special!

Thanks so much Ed, Erin and staff for all you did to make our son's party as wonderful as it was. Everything was perfect—the food, the room, the deck and the way it was so perfectly run. We are truly grateful, Mary & Ira

Thank you so much for making our wedding a wonderful event. It all ran so smoothly and everyone had a great time. The Orleans Inn will always hold a special place in our hearts.

Dear Ryan & your staff,

I would like to thank you for all your help and attention in making Carol and Eddies wedding reception a happy and successful time. It will be a memory they will always cherish.

To all: I want to thank you for the wonderful lunch at the Orleans Inn for some of the residents of Heatherwood. Everyone has commented that their choice of Lobster or Chicken Salad was outstanding and the service just great. You have made the Inn a very special place in a wonderful location of Town Cove. Thank you for making one of our outings so enjoyable. Judith Fisher Social Director

Dear Ed: On behalf of Nauset Regional Middle School I want to thank you for the great luncheon you served to our Nauset Pride students. The food was excellent and varied, the setting perfect and the extra touches you provided, such as presenting students with books, made it an outstanding event. Thank you very much for your support of our students and our school.

Dear Ed: On behalf of the Cape Cod Antique Dealers Association I would like to extend to you and your staff our sincere thanks and appreciation for our two annual holiday luncheons. The menu and service were excellent and the cost just right. In addition, the Orleans Inn has a certain ambiance that is about perfect for this part of Cape Cod.

Dear Orleans Inn staff, Thank you so much for helping to make my bridesmaid luncheon all the more special. Special thanks to Ryan for setting us up at a beautiful table on the deck. I truly appreciated the special touches. It was so nice for us to share part of our wedding experience with you. Marc and I will always remember working at the Inn with fondness. Thank you again!

Dear Ed, You are the best! Thank you for giving me the nicest wedding day a gal could have. Everything that you and your family & staff did to make it special meant so much to us. All my family & friends remarked at what a special place the Orleans Inn is and I think you'll have some repeat visitors! You have been on my mind and I thank you.

Dear Ed, Just a quick note to say "Thank you" for the fine lunch for the Orleans High reunion. We all enjoyed ourselves immensely and hope to see you next year for our 60th. Also thanks for the picture/plaque of the good old Orleans Inn which figured so largely in my youth. You are a great host and I enjoyed talking with you. Pray for our country! Sincerely, Father Franklin Darling

Dear Ryan, Just wanted to thank you and everyone who worked the afternoon of my parents 50th wedding anniversary. It couldn't have been more perfect! Everything went as planned. The food and service was excellent. Everyone had the best time. I'm so glad we had this special occasion at the Orleans Inn. My parents will never forget this party. Thank you so much for helping us make their 50th so special.

Dear Ryan and staff, I just had to write you to reiterate how fantastic we think you are. You created the most beautiful party for us. We, and our guests will never forget the warm hospitality, the cozy environment, the sensational food and the relaxed but efficient way in which you all worked. You're and incredible team and you need to know how very much you were appreciated. To have your spirit, coupled with a perfect evening, complete with the full moon—who could ask for more? Thank you all for adding to the joy of our wedding. We'll be back!

Dear Ed & staff at Orleans Inn, Thank you so much for a wonderful 40 birthday party. Ingrid et al put in extra touches & helped carry over the "Cape Cod—Summer" theme!

I had a wonderful time—just what I was hoping for—& my parents loved staying there, too! Thanks to all.

To the Staff at the Orleans Inn! Many thanks for making our day in Orleans such a pleasant one. As directors or volunteers of museums in other towns on the Cape, we enjoyed seeing Orleans in its Bicentennial Year. Lunch at the Orleans Inn and a tour of the Windmill finished off a busy day very nicely. The Cape & Islands Museum Assoc.

You have been so outstanding to work with over these past months, you made every request seem so simple. I cannot thank you enough for making this day come together with such ease and fun the way it should. Thank you from the bottom of my heart, you are wonderful.

Dear Ed, thank you for making Paul's 75th birthday celebration so wonderful. Everyone told us they had a great time! The food was delicious, and the service was perfect. Just a great evening. If we're all still around in five more years, maybe we'll do it again! Thanks once more for all your good efforts. Nancy

Dear Maas Family & Staff, Wanted to let you all know how much we enjoyed visiting your Inn for the Cape Chamber's gathering. The Inn looked festive and welcoming; the service genuine and sincere; and your gift certificates a surprise gift! Many Thanks, Chatham Wayside Inn Staff

Dear Ryan & Ed, Thank you very much for the wonderful time I had at the Annual Party hosted by you and your family and Polly and Wolfgang (Cape Cod Guide). What you have done with your Inn is truly remarkable and I can particularly appreciate it as I was interested in buying it and had toured it completely. The food was excellent and beautifully presented and your staff very courteous and helpful. I will not hesitate to recommend your lovely property for either dining or rooms to my guests and patrons. Thank you again for a lovely time. Mac, Colonial House Innkeeper

Dear Shannon, Thank you so very much for helping us have a wonderful and delicious general meeting last night. Everything was great. Orleans Chamber of Commerce

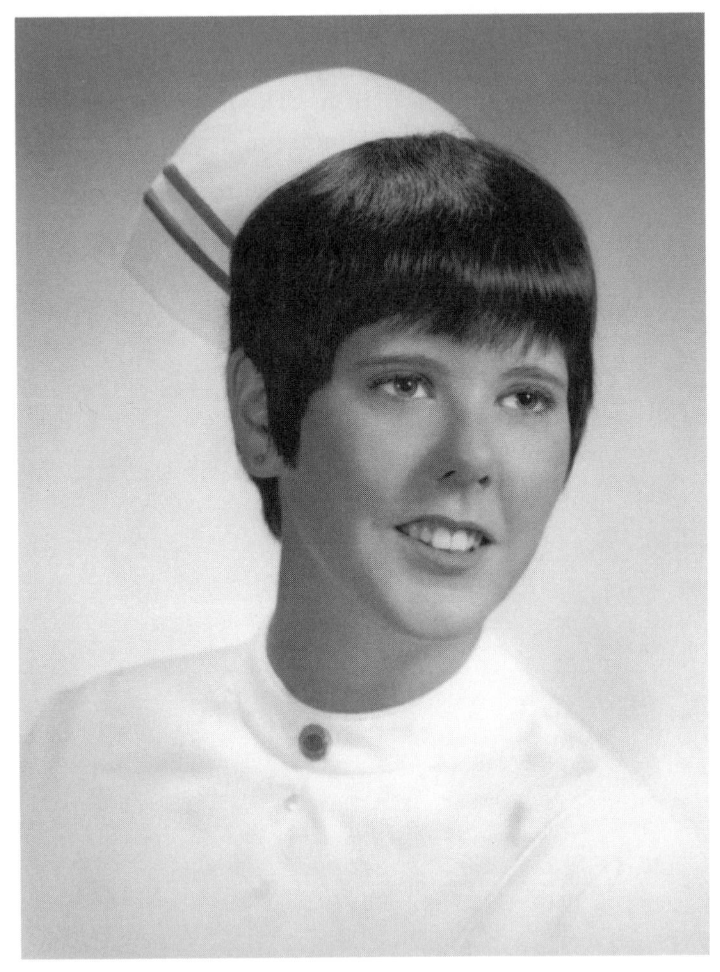

Laurie Gustafson Maas
Nursing School Graduation, Cape Cod Hospital, 1969

CHAPTER 21

FATE

Laurie and I feel we were meant to meet and spend the rest of our lives together. We have a picture from "It's a Wonderful Life" on display and so many people recognize and enjoy the meaning of that wonderful Jimmy Stewart film. So many things would have occurred differently if only one decision in life were changed. That one impulsive illogical decision we made to buy the Inn has brought meaning to many lives.

Growing up 1500 miles apart in totally different cultures made an interesting match. Ed will never forget the day he looked down the hallway at Parkway General Hospital and saw the most beautiful 22 year old critical care nurse and at the age of 19 gathered the courage to ask her to a party. "A pahty?" she asked. Not the bathroom, Ed said. They never went to the party but were married within a few months. Ed still loves the lack of R's where they should be and the insertion of R's where they shouldn't, but sounds great. Laurie went to Nursing

School at Cape Cod Hospital School of Nursing. She helped open the Cardiac ICU at South Shore Hospital. She then went to Miami Childrens Hospital and Parkway General Hospital. She is an RN III at Memorial Hospital in Pembroke Pines, FL

Their eight children have been a Godsend. If it were up to Laurie she would adopt another dozen. Ed says eight is enough and wait for the grandchildren. Laurie's sense of family was only reinforced when she found her birth mother. She was with her when she died and told her she did the right thing. Her mother Elizabeth was a strong influence in teaching Laurie to enjoy life and respect everyone. Great attributes for a Mom and nurse.

Laurie continues as a Critical Care Nurse at Memorial Hospital Pembroke. She has won many awards and is very dedicated. 2005 marks 30 years she has been caring for patients at the same hospital. She has touched thousands of lives and is well respected.

Ed has been greatly influenced by Laurie as well as his parents. Fred and Kay Maas taught all seven children the importance of faith and work ethic. Ed will never forget the kindnesses by his aunts and uncles. PJ and Pat O'Hagan will never be forgotten for the special memories they gave their nieces and nephews. Family is wonderful.

Ed could not have succeeded without the help of his little brother John. Ed will never forget the risk John and his older sister Carol took in assisting with the Inn. It is nice to have family that believes in your dreams. Kathleen and Mike Tyson are also to be recognized for their part in the Orleans Inn.

Ed and Laurie were taught as children the importance of their faith in God. This has delivered them through some very difficult times. Ed will never forget the 10 years teaching the CCD classes for Father Ed at St. Bonaventure Church. Ani McKee made it impossible for Ed to say no to assisting with the new parish and young families. He remembers with fondness the years spent as a Eucharistic Minister and teacher.

Ed chose healthcare over agriculture at the age of 16. This was partly because he was paid $1.25 an hour as opposed to 50 cents in the fields. It was a decision that brought him and Laurie together as well as ultimately to own the Inn. He worked seven days a week even while going to school and taking Honors courses. He became a college professor at Miami–Dade Community College at the age of 21 and 3 years later was the acting director of the Respiratory Therapy Program there. He became a hospital administrator at the age of 24. Walter Loebenberg owned US Healthcare and assisted Ed in developing the Maas Group. Ed transitioned from healthcare to hospitality gradually since 1996. Ed is now a member of the New England Resorts and Innkepers Association. He has continued to work seven days a week at the inn when Ryan left five years ago to become a manager for Back Bay Restaurant Group. He has established quite a reputation in the hospitality field. There was a tremendous void when Ryan left and it really impacted Ed.

Ed has become very comfortable in his role of Innkeeper. He is giving back to the community through volunteer work and fundraising for charitable organizations. He is inspired by the hard work and dedication of the twins and Josh. The best thing Erin brought home from Johnson&Wales was Josh who made it on his own as well. Josh is a wonderful and hardworking addition to the family. He is loved by staff and guests alike.

Ed and Laurie could not have succeeded without all of the wonderful people that have helped along the way. They include family, friends, clergy, staff and guests that have offered encouragement and support in this ambitious project.

EPILOUGE

We hope you have enjoyed this collection of stories on the Orleans Inn. We also hope you take advantage of the self guided tour of the Inn. This book will have most meaning for those that will visit the Inn to explore and enjoy its history. Even those that have visited the Inn in the past will have a fresh new perspective of the Grand Old Building.

We hope that you will have a chance to visit the Inn and in some way become a part of its future and history at the same time. The front door is always open although you may find Ed asleep on the couch. He is enjoying his fifth year of retirement spending every waking and sleeping hour at the Inn as well with the exception of an hour here or there to check on the house or to sneak away to Fort Hill.

Please stop in to share stories and enjoy the history. He would love to personally autograph the book for you as well as share some stories not suitable for print. We ask that you add your name and comments to our guest book which will remain in the Inn hopefully forever. Please feel free to browse through the noted names of past guests.

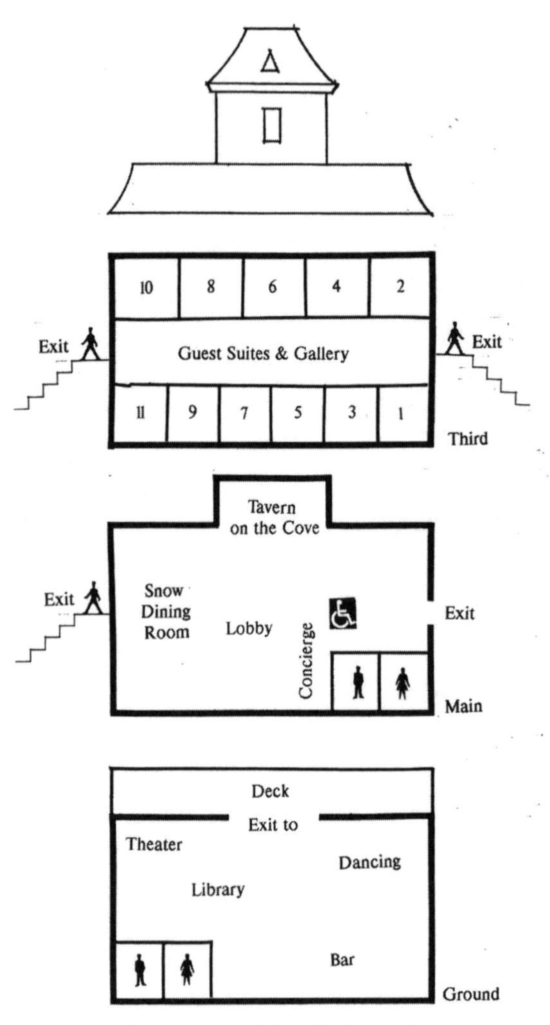

Floor Plan of the Orleans Inn

Self Guided Tour OF THE ORLEANS INN

After entering the solid mahogany doors of the 1875 sea captain mansion you should spend a few minutes in the foyer taking in the various paintings, plaques and awards on display. The Dining reviews and awards date almost every year the Inn has been operated by the Maas family. Also on display are crafts and photos given to the Maas family in recognition of the efforts to save the historic structure. Pirate maps of the area are also of interest. The curio cabinet offers an interesting display of articles including Ed's rare collection of antique candy containers. The glass shapes of cars, boats, trains, planes, etc. bring back fond memories of child anticipation of the candy beads enclosed in the toys.

❦

Enter the main lobby/living room and notice the hidden door built into the wall on the left. The picture frame wainscoting with marbleized wallpaper inserts and Victorian colors blend to conceal the entry to the hidden liquor room hiding the bootleg whiskey during Prohibition. It is now used as a coat room and entry to back office computers.

❦

Original oil paintings by Clifford Gustafson as well as an antique railroad map of Massachusetts depict the Cape prior to the canal adjoin the framed Masters Degree earned by Erin and Megan Maas. The MBA's are the first awarded to twins by Johnson&Wales University. The pen and ink illustration of the Inn was a gift from Architect Design who provided a tremendous amount of assistance with renovations.

❦

Follow the wall to the right towards the Concierge desk and you will pass the Roaring 20's flapper fringed lamp indicating the very colorful period of the Inn's history. Before moving on, notice the scissor shadow cut of the I Love New England poem. The wall behind the sofa holds another gift given us by the late Kathleen Bresnahan. She worked at the Inn and had a painting of the Inn during the period it was known as Inn of the Yankee Fisherman. Guests that knew the Inn during that period enjoy the painting.

❦

The reception desk displays an assortment of awards and photos including the Orleans Historical Society

Beautification Award presented to the Maas family for the restoration of the Inn. Harrad's Teddy Bears surround the lobby and dining room and provide the connection between Shawn Maas and British Literature. He brings his drama students to London for theater and brings back commemorative Harrad's Teddy Bears to the Inn.

❦

Brochures, maps and information are available at the Concierge desk. There is also a 90 second video depicting some of the beaches and adjacent parks. It also features a wedding held here 5/22/04. Heather and Brian were one of the special couples celebrating their wedding at the Inn. Heather's family owned the Inn when she was a child.

❦

Behind the desk is a Vernon Smith painting of the Inn from 1936. A tide clock is helpful with planned trips to the beach or fishing. The licenses on display include a signed $5 bill from Herbert Harrison our first customer. Although Herb passed away his family still owns Nauset Fish and Lobster Market across the street. We miss him and his memories.

❦

On display behind the second sofa is a large painting of the Inn by Jack Kitson. Feel free to take the postcard depictions of the painting. The portrait of Captain Aaron

Snow is above the list of Mayflower passengers including his ancestor Constance Hopkins, the teenage girl to first sight land across the cove known as the Nauset Highlands. Rockwell's Stockbridge at Christmas is below the portrait of Mary Snow mother of the seven Snow children. The Red Lion Inn at Stockbridge is similar to the Orleans Inn.

❦

Enter the hall to the rest rooms and enjoy the variety of pictures and plaques. The feature of the hallway is the Healthy Bottom Line a gift from the staff at Pembroke Pines General Hospital where Ed began an Obstetrics and Pediatrics unit when he was the Administrator. The theme follows through to the ladies room where there is a bassinette changing table and wash basin. There is also an antique telephone and stand. Take time to read the plaques for both meaning and humor. Laurie has selected her favorite messages.

❦

Enjoy the beautiful and magnificent fieldstone fireplace mantle. Above is a photograph of the Inn at sunrise by Wendell Welch. There is a family photo of Laurie and her late sister Sharon in a boat with her parents on the dock at Goose Hummock with the Inn in the background. It is from about 1955 and is a classic. The children found it in Laurie's scrapbook. The mantle becomes the feature of the Christmas decorations which transform the Inn from the day after Thanksgiving until New Years. The selection of antique hats and dolls are unique to the Inn. The dolls come from all over the world and the latest addition was acquired at the Christmas Markets in Germany.

❦

Proceed past the Hostess Stand to the O'Hagan Irish Pub and enjoy the full Victorian Back Bar. It is solid mahogany and was custom built for the Maas Family. Every seat has a view of the beautiful Town Cove. The antique Lionel Trains are on display from the micro-lam beams supporting the cathedral ceilings. Approximately 30 different beers are on display in addition to the seven beers on tap. Enjoy the paintings and plaques on display. The bar is fully stocked with premium liquors for your favorite cocktail.

❦

The hallway in front of the pub displays paintings and a special work by Clifford Gustafson. It is a very rare Rudyard Kipling poem on artists and was hand gilded in 1937 the year Kipling died. This painting was presented by Cliff as his Master's project at Boston University. It was always Laurie's favorite and was a gift from her mother, Betty.

Proceed through the door marked Guest Suites and Gallery. The 125th anniversary print of the painting by Jack Kitson is on display with many of his original works. Follow the mahogany stairs to the guest level and visit the uniquely decorated guest rooms. The doors will be open unless occupied and you are welcome to enter and enjoy the original photographs by Josue Santiago. Each room has private bath, refrigerator and cable TV. The suites also offer DVD and full size sleeper sofas. Each room has a book of memories that contain some very personal reflections of past guests. Enjoy reading them.

❦

Notice the antique school desk at the stairs leading to the 5 room family suite on the mansard level. There is another flight leading to the Belvedere which contains a dining area. The last level or 6th floor is the Cupola and has a Christmas tree year round. This was a welcoming tradition to the returning sailors. The captain built this level as a look out for his ship the Nettie M. Rogers. This level was known in some sea captain mansions as a widow's walk. The triangle windows offer a spectacular look at the Atlantic Ocean. It is easier to proceed down the stairs the way you came up or backwards.

❦

At the main level you will sea the guest book which you are invited to sign and view photos in the scrapbook of the Inn. Above is a Sailors Valentine from the Cahoon Museum. Next you will see a magnificent Victorian Christening Gown. It is from the same period of the construction of the Inn in the late 1800's. Above the stairs is our Victorian Angel. She watches over the Inn continuously.

❦

Below her is the original oil painting by Karen North Wells Lunch at Nauset. It is a classic and is familiar to many guests that have visited Nauset Beach. Prints of the Swan Boats in Boston Gardens and the Grist Mill in Brewster are favorites.

❦

Proceed into the Snow Dining Room and enjoy the feel of the rich mahogany booths and unique round tables for 10. These were custom built for us as the Inn has become such a special occasion place there was demand for larger parties which we try to accommodate.

❦

The works of Clifford Gustafson and Laurie's maternal grandfather Arthur Long are on display in the dining room. The paintings of the Smith Cottage on Rock Harbor Road are almost 100 years old. They were recently acquired as a gift from a family member. Arthur was the art teacher at Brockton High and painted with Cliff in the summer. One of Cliff's paintings of Rockport recently returned to the family after being sold at an antique art dealer in New Hampshire. The owner displayed it in their living room and was told that Clifford Gustafson's works were on display at the Orleans Inn. They delivered it to the Inn and enjoyed the hospitality of the Maas family in appreciation.

❦

The Baby Grand player piano is the center of attention situated between the massive fieldstone fireplace and the German Grandfather Clock. The Curio display has items from the Portobello market in London. The engagement figure is from Edinborough, Scotland.

The wait kitchen is available to guests for refreshments 24 hours a day. It also is where guests help themselves to breakfast from 7 until 10am daily.

❦

Please visit the historic Jonathon Young Windmill Park adjacent to the Inn. It is an actual working windmill on a hill overlooking the Cove. It is a beautiful site for weddings.

❦

Goose Hummock is a tradition on Cape Cod. Visit the outdoor sporting center once owned by former Massachusetts Governor William Sargent. Mike McAskill, the current owner has been responsible for developing the business into the best on Cape Cod.

Gallery Tour

Jack Kitson was born in Stroudsburg, PA and earned a Bachelor of Science in Art Education from Kutztown University. For a time he lived in Marblehead and operated the Front Street Art Gallery. Since moving to the Cape his artwork has been selected seven times for the Wellfleet Guide Book Cover. As a freelance commercial artist, he has done work for Allstate, Avon, Goya and Rock Resorts. In 1997 he designed the set for Edward Albee's Pulitzer Prize winning play, "Seascape", performed in Provincetown. Original art and prints are available at the Studio/Gallery, 20 Massasoit Rd., Eastham. 508-255-6426

His work is also on exhibit throughout Cape Cod.

Enter the Gallery through the door Marked Gallery and Guest Suites. The gallery is on the same level as the guest suites on level above the lobby.

1A "EASTHAM"

This is a view of the Eastham Coast Guard Station. The area in the foreground is part of Nauset Marsh where people sail the boats and kayacks today. Many waterfowl are found here also.

1B "EASTHAM FOOTBRIDGE"

Two hiking trails begin at the Eastham Coast Guard Station—bicycles can be used as well.

7 "LIETENANT ISLAND BRIDGE"

A Wellfleet Secret–At high tide the bridge is impassable. Many birds and waterfowl are found here and few people.

11 "EASTHAM WINDMILL"

Located on the village green, this windmill is open to the public in the spring and summer and during "Windmill Weekend".

12 "HEMENWAY LANDING"

This depicts the Eastham Coast Guard Station in the distance with the artist in the canoe.

13 "EASTHAM LIGHT"

'Nauset Light' was only 60 feet from the cliff before it was moved back. An average of 3 feet per year is lost to erosion.

14 "WHALES-BALLENAS"

Humpback whales travel from the North to the South and back.

15 "CAPE TIP STREET"

This picture is also called 'tipsy street-a view of Provincetown'

16 "COMMERCIAL STREET WELLFLEET

This artwork appeared on the cover of the 1986

Wellfleet Book. Some artistic license was used to convey the real character of the town.

17 "UNCLE TIM'S BRIDGE"

A must visit in Wellfleet is to walk over the bridge and turn around to photograph the ridge with the Congregational Church in the background.

18 "MORNING GLORY"

This artwork appeared on the 1995 Wellfleet Book. In the distance you can see Indian Neck and Great Island as well as Wellfleet Harbor. Morning Glory is the name of the house and was constructed with parts from an old Wellfleet windmill.

19 "THE LOBSTER HUT"

This artwork appeared in the 1990 Wellfleet Book. Uncle Tim's bridge can be seen on the far right.

20 "COMMERCIAL STREET, WELLFLEET"

This artwork appeared on the cover of the 1986 Wellfleet Book. The Customs House has been renovated. The Masonic Hall has retained its character.

21 "WELLFLEET SKYLINE"

This artwork appeared on the cover of the 1985 Wellfleet Book. When you travel on Route 6—look left after the Wellfleet traffic light and you will see a salt marsh pond with wild ducks.

22 "EAST MAIN STREET, WELLFLEET"

When you turn left from Route 6 you will see the front side view of the "Wellfleet Skyline".

23 “MAIN STREET”

This artwork appeared on the cover of the 2001 Wellfleet Book. My good friend ‘Myra’ is walking her dog.

4 “MAP”

1720 Map of Cape Cod—Historical research by the artist provides a unique perspective of the changing shoreline and indigenous Indian names and facts.

24 “WELLFLEET CHURCHES”

The Congregational Church and Methodist Church are both located on Main Street. Snow is beautiful sometimes.

25 “DUTCH CITY ON THE AMSTEL”

This painting is a version of a Rembrandt style view of the River Amstel.

26 “DUTCH WHALER”

The Dutch were the first to go great distances in search of whales.

27 “WHALING, 1765”

When the blubber was removed from the dead whale it was brought aboard ship and cooked on deck to render ‘whale oil’ which provided fuel for lighting.

28 “THE GOLDEN HIND”’

This ship was the first to successfully travel around the treacherous Cape Horn of South America.

29 “PROVINCETOWN SKYLINE”

Provincetown harbor offers excellent protection of its beaches, boaters and houses built on the waters edge.

30 “SINGLE PORTHOLE CATBOAT”

Catboats were built sturdy and could handle tough waves and wind.

31 “TRIPLE PORTHOLE CATBOAT”

Variations were made to many boats, however basic design remained the same.

32 “DENNIS VILLAGE GREEN”

The town bandstand is a popular location—next to the Dennis Union Church.

33 “YARMOUTHPORT VILLAGE GREEN”

The Swedish Church faces the historic route 6A—many side streets here are just as interesting. The village green is host to special events and is a great place to just sit outside in the summer.

AS YOU WALK DOWN THE STAIRS NOTICE THE MAGNIFICENT PAINTING OF THE THREE GHOSTS KNOWN TO RESIDE AT THE INN.

GOODNIGHT!!!
!!!!!!!!!!!!!!!!!!!!!!!!!!!!!!!!!!!

ORLEANS INN
Menu

Appetizers

Orleans Inn Clam Chowder

Orleans Inn Lobster Bisque

Scallops Wrapped in Bacon

Maine Crab Cakes

With a chili-lime sauce and marinated cucumbers

Warm Lobster Dip

Served with seasoned pita chips

Nacho Platter
With pepperoncini, black olives, diced tomatoes,
melted Monterrey Jack and cheddar cheese

Chicken & Portabella Quesadilla
Diced chicken, portabella mushrooms,
Caramelized onions and cheddar cheese

Buffalo Chicken Tenders
Boneless chicken tenders tossed in hot sauce and served with Bleu cheese and celery on the side

Onion Rings

Orleans Inn Pizza

Roasted red peppers, shallots, olives, Tomatoes, pepperoncini, Monterrey Jack and cheddar cheese

Chicken Tenders

With honey mustard or barbeque sauce

Lobster Filled Raviolis

Served with a lobster cream sauce

Shrimp Cocktail

Fried Calamari

With pepperoncini, red peppers and marinara sauce

Warm Crab Dip

Served with seasoned pita chips

Chicken Nacho Platter

Grilled chicken breast, pepperoncini, black olives, diced tomatoes, melted Monterrey Jack and cheddar cheese

Vegetarian Quesadilla

Caramelized onions, red peppers, portabella mushrooms, & cheddar cheese

Jumbo Chicken Wings

Buffalo style, hot or mild served with blue cheese and celery on the side

Potato Skins

Filled with bacon and cheese

Mushroom and Cheese Pizza

Marinara sauce, portabella mushrooms, Monterrey Jack and cheddar cheese

Orleans Inn Appetizer Sampler

Potato skins, onion rings and chicken tenders

Oysters, Clams, Steamers or Mussels

Market price, when available

Salads

Duck Salad

Shredded duck, chevre cheese, & pecans with a sherry mustard vinaigrette

House Salad

Red onions, tomatoes, parmesan cheese, croutons and balsamic vinaigrette

Spinach Salad

With pine nuts, feta cheese and yellow Tomato vinaigrette

Caesar Salad

Romaine lettuce, shredded parmesan cheese, croutons all tossed in our Caesar dressing

Add chicken to any salad

Add shrimp to any salad

Entrees

11/4 lb. Steamed Native Lobster

Served with rice pilaf and vegetables

Grilled North Atlantic Salmon

With an orange honey glaze sauce
Served with rice pilaf and vegetables

Stuffed Sole

Spinach and cheese stuffed sole
With a lobster cream sauce
Served with rice pilaf and vegetables

Fried Clam Platter

Whole belly clams served with fries and coleslaw

Sea Scallop Platter

Fried-served with fries and coleslaw

Or Broiled served with rice and vegetables

Fish and Chips

Lightly breaded and fried cod

Served with fries and coleslaw

Cape Cod Seafood Trio

Fried scallops, clams and cod

Served with fries and coleslaw

Chicken Piccata

Sautéed chicken breast with lemon,

Capers and shallots served with rice pilaf and vegetables

***New York Sirloin**

12oz sirloin with herbed garlic butter,

Mashed potatoes and vegetables

***Orleans Inn Prime Rib of Beef**

With mashed potatoes and vegetables

Pastas

Chicken Parmesan

Italian breaded chicken breast baked with our special marinara sauce and melted cheese served over linguini

Shrimp Pesto Pasta

Sautéed shrimp with a pesto-cream Sauce served over linguini

Spicy Sautéed Calamari

Served over linguini with marinara sauce, pepperoncini, black olives and tomatoes

Vegetarian Selection

Wild mushroom raviolis with a pesto-cream sauce and parmesan cheese

Sandwiches

All sandwiches served with a choice of French Fries, coleslaw or Cape Cod Potato Chips

Lobster Salad Sandwich

On a toasted hotdog roll

Fried Fish Sandwich

Fried cod served on a toasted bulkie roll

Turkey Club

With bacon, lettuce and tomato served On white Texas toast

Buffalo Chicken Wrap

With lettuce and bleu cheese

Chicken Salad Sandwich

On a toasted bulkie roll with diced Bacon, red onions and chives

****Orleans Inn Angus Burger***

On a toasted bulkie roll served with Lettuce, tomato and red onions

Fried whole-belly Clam Roll

On a toasted hotdog roll

Fried Scallop Roll

On a toasted hotdog roll

Grilled Chicken Sandwich

With bacon and melted Swiss cheese

On a bulkie roll with lettuce & tomato

Turkey Sandwich Wrap

With cheddar cheese, cranberry sauce and tomatoes in a flour tortilla wrap

Hot Pastrami and Swiss

On Pumpernickel with lettuce & tomato

Vegetarian Burger

On a bulkie roll with cheddar cheese, Caramelized onions, lettuce & tomato

Additional Toppings for Sandwiches

Bacon, Caramelized Onions, Portabella Mushrooms, Roasted Red Peppers,

American cheese, Swiss cheese, Cheddar Cheese

**Cooked to order. Consuming of raw or undercooked meats and fish may increase your risk of food borne illnesses, especially if you have certain medical conditions.*

ORLEANS INN
Dessert Menu

Strawberry Cheesecake
A combination of strawberries and New York style cheesecake
In a graham cracker crust, garnished with whipped cream
Triple Layer Chocolate Cake
The ultimate chocolate delight!
A layer of chocolate mousse and a layer of chocolate butter cake
Topped with a rich chocolate ganache and whipped cream
Kentucky Bourbon Pecan Pie
Large buttery caramel pecans with a hint of Bourbon
On top of a butter short bread crust, garnished with whipped cream
Raspberry Crème Brulee
Key Lime Pie
This refreshingly light pie is made with zesty key lime juice
And baked in a graham cracker crust, topped with real whipped cream
Warm Apple Crisp
served with vanilla ice-cream, caramel sauce and whipped cream
Brownie Sundae
chocolate chip brownie topped with vanilla ice cream,
whipped cream and chocolate sauce
Ice cream
Chocolate, Vanilla or Coffee

ORLEANS INN
Brunch Menu

Special Omelets

Served with breakfast potatoes and toast

Orleans Inn Omelet

Roasted red peppers, shallots, olives, tomatoes, pepperoncini, and cheese

Cape Cod Omelet

Lobster meat, shallots, tomatoes and cheese

Skaket Omelet

Ham, tomatoes, mushrooms, shallots and cheese

Nauset Omelet

Bacon, roasted red peppers, shallots and cheese

Town Cove Omelet

Crab meat, roasted red peppers, shallots and cheese

Create Your Own Omelet

Choose any of your favorite toppings.........

Cheese, Red Peppers, Tomatoes, Shallots, Mushrooms, Bacon, Ham, Capers, pepperoncini

Extras

Berries and Cream

Fresh berries and whipped cream

Irish Banger Style Sausages

Side of Bacon

Side of Breakfast Potatoes

Breakfast Specialties

Orleans Inn Eggs Benedict

Two poached eggs served over ham and an English muffin with a Hollandaise sauce served with breakfast potatoes

Lobster Eggs Benedict

Two poached eggs served over lobster meat and an English muffin with a lobster cream sauce served with breakfast potatoes

Spinach Eggs Benedict

Two poached eggs served over spinach and an English muffin with a Hollandaise sauce served with breakfast potatoes

Orleans Inn French Toast

Served with breakfast potatoes

Bacon Egg & Cheese Roll-up

In a white flour tortilla served with breakfast potatoes

Scrambled Eggs & Bacon

Served with breakfast potatoes & toast

Egg Club Sandwich

Turkey, bacon, eggs and cheese on a bulkie roll with breakfast potatoes

ORLEANS INN

Recipe Selection

Orleans Inn Lobster Salad

Serves 6

2 pounds fresh lobster meat

3ounces Mayonaise

1/4 ounce chives

1/4 lemon (use strainer)

Mix all ingredients

Serve in grilled buttered roll or over mixed greens

ORLEANS INN
Portfolio

INTERCONTINENTAL.
HOTELS GROUP

November 22, 2004

Mr. Ed Maas
Owner
The Orleans Inn
21 Rt. 6A, Po Box 188
Orleans, Ma. 02653

Dear Ed,

I would just like to take this opportunity to thank you, your family and staff for the outstanding service you all provided my family and myself during our time of need while in Orleans last week.

As someone who grew up in the area and with the exception of the last 10 years, my family has been part of Orleans for over 130 years, it was refreshing to meet someone who still operates a business based on trust and respect. You made us feel at home from the moment we arrived. The staff knew us quickly and went out of their way to show an extra smile and attend to all our needs.

As someone who has been in the hotel business for over 25 years, this is a welcome and refreshing change. Thanks again for everything you did and it's great to see an old landmark like The Orleans Inn revived and vibrant once again.

Have a safe and happy Holiday Season.

Sincerely,

Neil J. Flavin
Regional Director
Crowne Plaza Hotels & Resorts
Intercontinental Hotels Group

Orleans Inn was featured in the 2003 Annual Report for Royal Bank of Scotland which was sent all over the world.

PAGE 8 THE CAPE CODDER FRIDAY, MAY 25, 2001 www.capecodder.com

CAPE PORTRAITS

Erin Maas: Young woman in the inn

By Jeffrey S. Hyer

For most high school marketing projects, most students pick T-shirts, pens or coffee mugs to sell to fellow students, but not Erin Maas. She chose a multimillion dollar inn to promote to the world.

What began as a simple idea for a school project five years ago turned into an award winning entry that eventually led Maas down a career path she did not expect to take. Today, the 21-year-old is headed into the fast-paced world of hotel and restaurant management.

The choice of marketing an inn was an easy one. Her father, Ed Mass, had just purchased the Orleans Inn in 1996 as an investment. Wanting to learn more about what dad just paid for, Maas and her fraternal twin sister, Megan, chose the inn for a high school marketing competition. The project won a state competition and a college scholarship.

Maas grew up with her four brothers and three sisters in Fort Lauderdale, Fla., where the family still has a home. After the purchase of the inn, the family was spending its holidays, vacations and summers running the inn and the rest of the time in Florida. Maas began working the hostess stand at the inn during her junior year in high school. She didn't know it at the time, but she had slipped into a career in the hospitality industry.

"I wasn't really sure what I wanted to do in high school, but I knew after I began working in this business," she said. What clinched her decision was the winning marketing plan and the scholarship.

Erin Maas

Staff photo by Jeffrey S. Hyer

Last week, she completed her third year at the Hospitality College at Johnson and Wales University's Providence, R.I., campus, where she is majoring in hotel and restaurant management.

Using knowledge gleaned from her education, for the past year she has helped in the hiring and management of employees for the inn, which has 11 rooms and a 200-seat pub and restaurant, plus a function room.

She said she is a stickler for details, which is important to please patrons.

"The most important aspect of this job is that you have to have the personality to deal with different types of customers, meeting all of their expectations," she said. "I am the type of person that wants to make everybody happy."

Erin's boyfriend, Josh Santiago, who also is pursuing a degree in hospitality and attends classes with her, said her ability to please people comes naturally.

"She is focused on people and in this business you have to be very good at that," he said. "She wants to make sure everybody is happy, which includes both employees and customers."

Maas has taken advantage of using school projects and her professors' knowledge and combining them with needed undertakings for the family business. Last year, she began working on a personnel and policy manual as part of a requirement for one of her management classes. Instead of using textbook facts and figures, she used the inn's actual situation to develop manuals on improving service that have been put in practice this spring. She received a perfect score on the project.

"There was a lot of stuff we were missing," she said. "By using my textbooks and with help from my professor, we were able to begin improving our service."

Her father is happy with his daughter's career choice and is happy to have the burgeoning professional help.

"She just really took this thing and went with it," he said. "She wanted to become involved."

While her siblings work at the inn, Erin is the only one who is attending school for hospitality. Two of her siblings are teachers, her fraternal twin is interested in marketing, and a brother is learning business management.

While Maas credits a lot of her knowledge of hotel and restaurant management to her schooling, she said there is no better educational method than hands-on. "The best way of learning is by doing, and every day I learn something new when I am working here."

Her most enjoyable aspect of the job is working with the other employees and talking with the guests, but the long hours that people management involves is her least favorite part of the business. During the summer, Maas often works from 9 a.m. to midnight, seven days a week. But, she said, "The long hours aren't that bad when you are working with people who are close to you."

As part of her commitment to her education and the hospitality industry, Maas was recently awarded a $20,000 KOPF Foundation Wine and Food scholarship. This national scholarship is given to just five students annually. In late August, Maas will spend seven weeks touring wineries in California, France and Italy, where she will assist in grape harvesting, learn about the art of making wine, tour production facilities, and be taught tasting techniques.

THE CAPE CODDER FRIDAY, MARCH 1, 2002 PAGE 2

ORLEANS

AROUND TOWN

The winner is ...

Orleans Inn owner Ed Maas, left, accepts the Orleans Chamber of Commerce Community Service award from chamber President Ken Alman during a brief ceremony at the inn Thursday morning. The award, based on extraordinary service to the community by an individual, business or organization, is the first by the chamber. Standing in the background, from left, are Kyle Hinkle, Nick Pangakis, Scott Rogers, Judy Hunt and Sherri Mahoney.

Staff photo by Merrily Lunbsford

ABOUT THE AUTHOR

Edward J. Maas was born in Homestead, FL on September 30, 1952. He graduated from South Dade High School in 1970 and Miami-Dade Community College in 1972. He received his BS in 1974 and MPA in 1976 from Florida International University. He became a registered respiratory therapist and then a hospital administrator. He is CEO of the Maas Group, a healthcare consulting and hospitality management company.

Maas was honored by the City of Hope and the Palm Beach County Medical Society. He has spent the past decade saving the historic structure known as the Orleans Inn.

Beginning in third person narrative, he drifts to first person experiences and back. Thousands of guests have suggested he write a book about the experience of saving the Inn. Please join Ed in his love of history and the Orleans Inn.

Publication of this book was underwritten by
Maas Group Inc.
a Florida Corporation
and
Orleans Waterfront Inn
a Massachusetts Corporation.

Cover Art
By Jackson Taylor Kitson
P.O. 691 Eastham, MA 02642
www.barnside.com/beachesgallery